DARGER'S RESOURCES

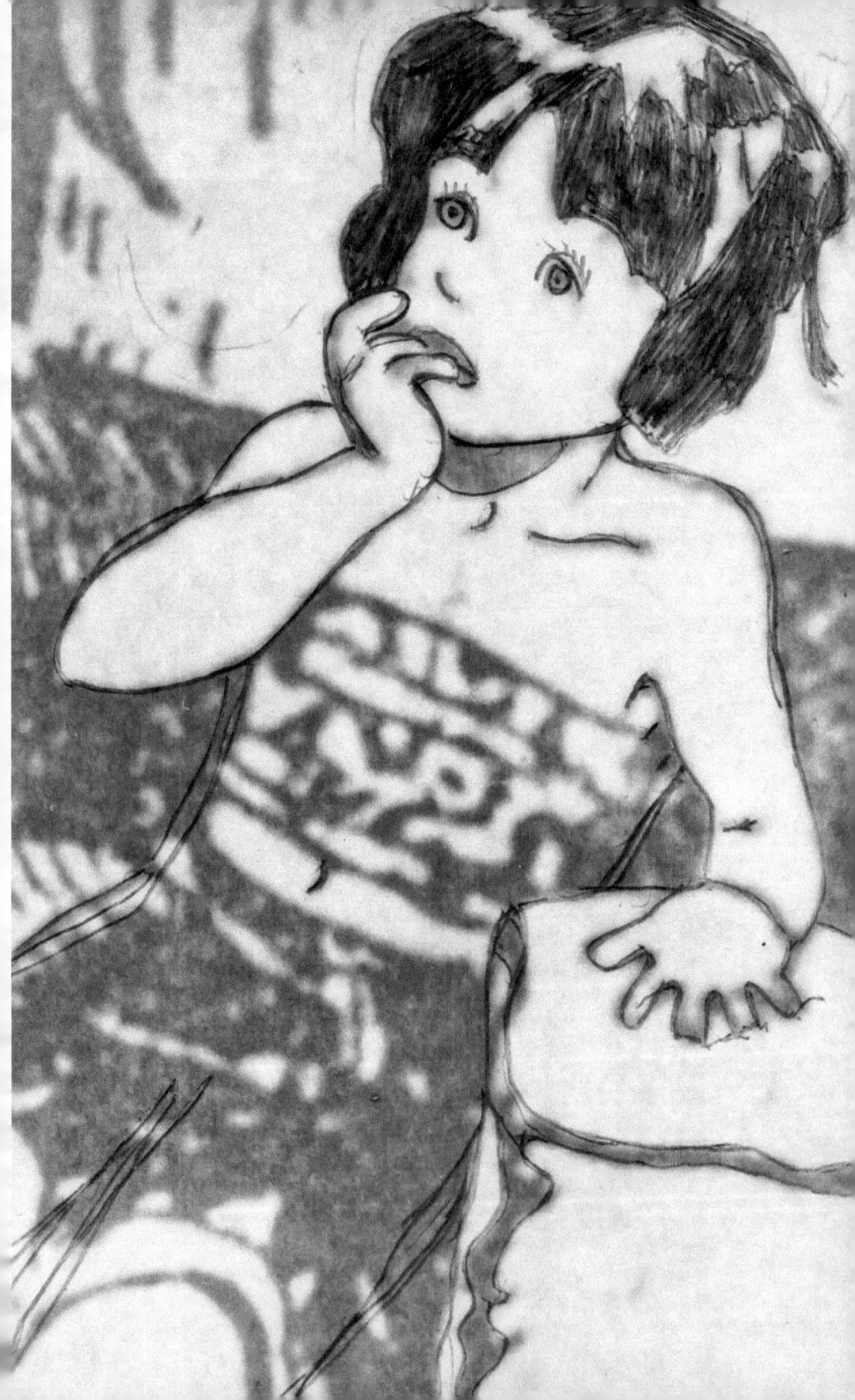

MICHAEL MOON   **DARGER'S RESOURCES**

Duke University Press

DURHAM AND LONDON

2012

Duke University Press gratefully acknowledges the support of
the College of Arts and Sciences, and the James T. Laney School
of Graduate Studies, both at Emory University, which provided
funds toward the production of this book.

Designed by Amy Ruth Buchanan
Typeset in Quadraat by Tseng Information Systems, Inc.
Library of Congress Cataloging-in-Publication Data appear
on the last printed page of this book.

Frontispiece: Darrell McClure. "Little Annie Rooney."
Newspaper clipping altered by Darger from the collection
of Henry Darger. Collection American Folk Art Museum,
New York. © Kiyoko Lerner 2003.

To the memory of **HENRY DARGER,**
with gratitude and admiration, and
yet once more to **JONATHAN GOLDBERG,**
with thanks, as Setsuko Hara says in
Ozu's *Late Spring*, for these years.

CONTENTS

When I first started studying Henry Darger's work in earnest about a decade ago, there was a lot of heat around the question of whether he might have perpetrated the kinds of acts he depicts in some passages of his writings and in his paintings that show children being strangled and eviscerated by sadistic adults. During the years since, some needful breathing space has opened up, in which most of those who write about the work seem less inclined to take the depiction of a fantasy as evidence of the commission of an act, or even of the intention to commit it. It is my hope that this book may contribute to the consideration of Darger as someone who, by virtue of his massive and lifelong project of writing and art, took on the role of witness to the terrible ordinariness of violence in the history of the twentieth century—especially violence against children, and specifically against girls.

Much of the public discourse around Darger of a decade ago proceeded in a fairly tight loop between points of paranoid suspicion: on the one hand, in paying attention to and enjoying Darger's work, might we (after the fact, anyway) somehow be aiding and abetting a pedophile serial killer, either actual or would-be? On the other hand is the defensive response, which often says that to appear to be obsessed with certain forms of violence does not necessarily mean that one is bound to enact them, or even wants to. Given the intensity of the particular combination of violence and vulnerability at the core of Darger's work—children martyred in wartime—the debate around whether we should dismiss that work on ethical grounds as itself a series of acts of extreme violence may have been an inevitable stage in its early reception. But given the focus of so much of the initial discussion of the work on the question of its possible moral indefensibility, it has been particularly gratifying to see it more recently receiving some of the attention and respect usually accorded only to "classic" works of art and literature.

Until very recently, for example, it is hard to imagine a classics scholar such as Mark Payne (in his recent *Theocritus and the Invention of Fiction* [Cambridge: Cambridge University Press, 2007]) introducing his main topic, the early history of the production of highly developed fictive worlds in poetry, with an opening chapter titled, after Darger's epic saga, "In the Realms of the Unreal," and adducing Darger's work in elaborate detail in the first several pages of his book as a particularly rich and compelling instance of the disruption of ontological boundaries between real and imaginary worlds of the kind Payne's book addresses. Comparably striking is the Italian philosopher Giorgio Agamben's treatment of Darger in his *Ninfe* (also 2007), in which one chapter relates Darger's "nymphs" to questions about the depiction and theorization of similar figures in early Italian Renaissance art and in the early twentieth-century writing of the art historian Aby Warburg.

It was Warburg who first raised the question of what he called the *Pathosformel*, the "feeling formula," the combination of means by which (as he saw it) earlier artists had invented visual figures that were for themselves and their more responsive viewers saturated with emotional cues and meanings. A central one of these figures for Warburg's investigations was that of the nymph, a figure developed in art of the classical era that was revived and, according to Warburg, reinvested with complex combinations of intense affect by artists of the early Renaissance. Warburg first wrote about the figure of the nymph and its possible meanings in a mock correspondence he initiated with a friend (named André Jolles), the generative conceit of which was that Jolles has fallen deeply in love with the dancing servant girl (Warburg's first nymph) who appears in Ghirlandaio's *Nativity of John the Baptist* fresco in the Church of Santa Maria Novella in Florence (fig. 1). For Jolles (and for Warburg after him)—or, rather, for the bedazzled, torturously and ecstatically lovelorn persona they invent together and on whom they project their shared fascination with her—Ghirlandaio's serving girl somehow em-

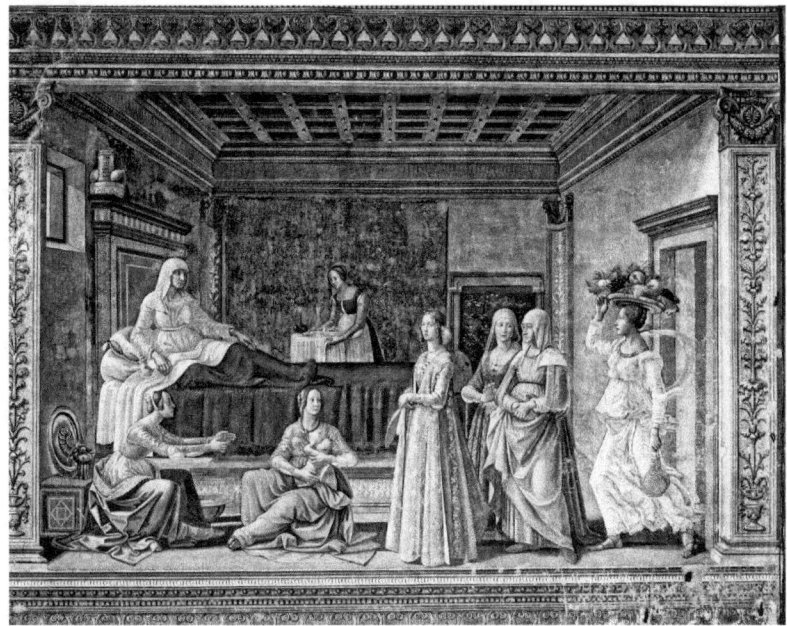

FIGURE I. Domenico Ghirlandaio (1448–94). *Nativity of John the Baptist* (Santa Maria Novella, Florence, Italy). Photo Credit: Scala / Art Resource, NY.

blematizes and compresses into herself many of their other favorite artistic figures. Warburg writes:

> In many of the works of art I had always liked, I discovered something of my Nymph. My condition varied between a bad dream and a fairy tale. . . . Sometimes she was Salome dancing . . . ; sometimes she was Judith carrying [Holofernes's head] . . . ; then again she appeared to hide in the boy-like grace of little Tobias. . . . Sometimes I saw her in a seraph flying towards God in adoration and then again in a Gabriel announcing the good tidings. I saw her as a bridesmaid expressing innocent joy . . . and again as a fleeing mother, the terror of death in her face, at the Massacre of the Innocents.
>
> I began to lose my reason. It has always been she who brought life and movement into an otherwise calm scene. Indeed, she appeared to be the very embodiment of movement.[1]

A reader familiar with Darger's work—especially one who has encountered Agamben's discussion of what he calls the *Nympha dargeriana*—may be struck with how strongly and at how many different points this early evoca-tion of the Pathosformel of the nymph resonates with fundamental aspects of Darger's art and writing: in the strangely mixed atmosphere of nightmare and fairy tale that pervades the work, especially in the figure of the girl, at once a charming and seductive dancer and a ruthless and ferocious warrior (Salome and Judith)—and yet a girl who is in some of her most "grace[ful]" manifestations gendered male (the boy Tobias), but who at other moments also manifests herself as winged seraph and archangel (like the Blengins, also called Blengiglomeneans, the winged dragon spirits who guard Darger's Vivian Girls and their child comrades).

One of the most captivating (and pathetic) expressions of this figure, the young woman in highly expressive motion, is that of the terrified and grief-stricken young mother who sees her infant seized and murdered by soldiers. As "the Massacre of the Innocents"—the slaughter of all newborn males in Bethlehem ordered by King Herod in order to eliminate the infant King of the Jews the Magi told him about—this scene has been a central topos of Christian art. Indeed, in the Ghirlandaio cycle in Santa Maria Novella, just across the chapel from the *Nativity of John the Baptist*, with the serving nymph who so captivated and stimulated Warburg, there is a *Massacre of the Innocents* (fig. 2), the tumultuous and bloody scene that is one of the small number of scenes that constitute the canon of the iconography of the nativity of Jesus. A series of just such massacres, as reimagined by Darger in the context of his Glandeco-Angelinian War Storm, are integral to his project. The relative modernity of Darger's versions of this scene manifests itself in the quasi-scientific anatomical detail with which he sometimes depicts the mutilation of the children's bodies in his visual images of slaughters of the innocent. But his indestructible nymphs, the seven Vivian Girls, successfully escape massacre even as he represents their frequent extreme peril in the strange and striking image of them dashing about, nymphlike, among their crucified sister warriors.

If the discourses around Darger's work initially emphasized his own al-leged psychopathology as the source of the violence and the other gener-ally disturbing qualities of some of his work, scholarship such as that of Payne, Agamben, and Warburg suggests much broader and deeper contexts in which to explore the significance and meaning of that work. The focus of the present book is not on the roots of Darger's work in ancient and early modern art and literature, but on its extensive sources (some of Darger's most reliable resources) in twentieth-century mass culture. Nonetheless,

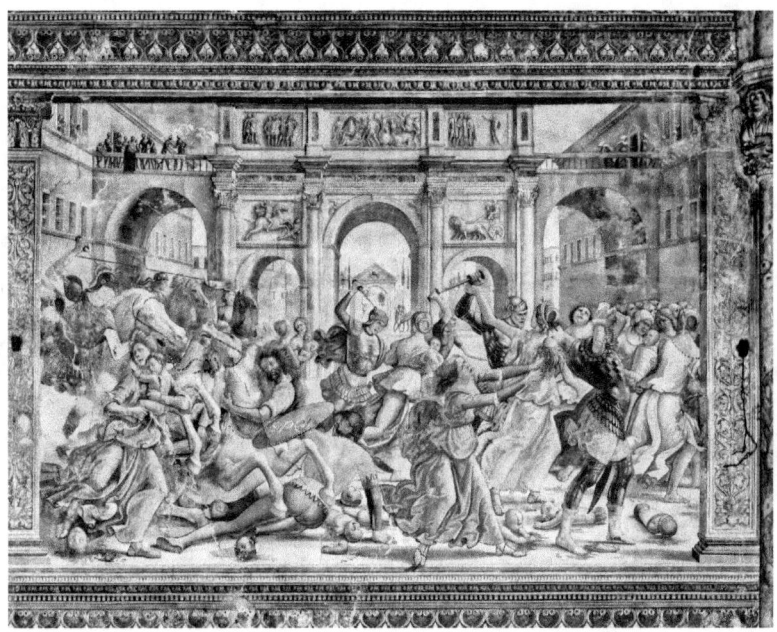

FIGURE 2. Domenico Ghirlandaio. *Massacre of the Innocents* (Santa Maria Novella, Florence, Italy). Photo Credit: Scala / Art Resource, NY.

to someone like myself who has concentrated primarily on the relations of Darger's work to such media as newspaper comic strips, pulp fiction, and mass-produced religious art, the advent of this other new Darger scholarship on the ancient and early modern counterparts of his work is highly encouraging.

This new direction in scholarship that determinedly shifts the contexts for Darger's work away from John Wayne Gacy and Jeffrey Dahmer—and even, to a considerable degree, from the category of "outsider art" altogether—constitutes a departure that one can see already being signaled in some of Darger's own productions. I think, for example, of a typically monumental watercolor (32″ x 132″) of his, *Untitled (The Arcadeia)* (fig. 3). It depicts a characteristically busy and crowded domestic interior, an extended, complex space thronged with little girls and a few guardian Blengins (distinguished by their rams' horns). At the center of the composition a group of girls poses on an elevated platform, while a larger group gathers in front of them; many figures in both groups (again characteristically) gaze outward from the picture space, making potential eye contact with the viewer. In the

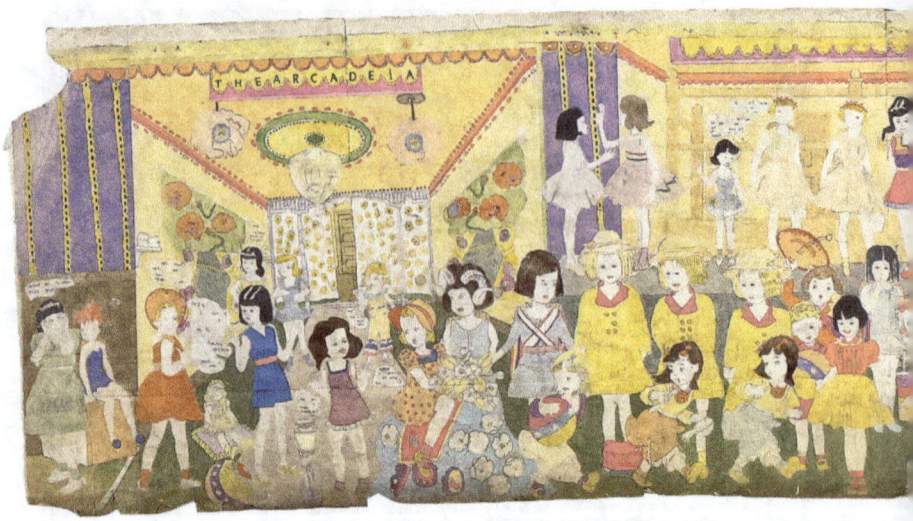

FIGURE 3. Henry Darger (1892–1973). Untitled *(The Arcadeia)*.
Copyright Kiyoko Lerner, courtesy of Andrew Edlin Gallery.

right-hand third of the picture, yet another group of children stand before a picture window, through which the viewer can see a half-dozen girls, most of them bearing open umbrellas, contending with the heavy winds and rain of a thunderstorm. By way of contrast, the left-hand side of the picture shows a room extending far back, away from the frontal surface of the picture. There are a dozen or so figures arrayed at or near the front of the space, but otherwise it (unlike any other space in the picture) is uninhabited—as uninhabited as it is highly decorated. What distinguishes it from the rest of the spaces pictured here are such conspicuous touches as two massive flower-shades on the ceiling lights, the billowing curtains—festooned with giant pansies and purple blossoms—at the two side windows (through both of which the rainstorm outside is visible), and the floor-length, yellow-blossom curtains that cover the space at the rear of the image. At the top front of the space, Darger has labeled the room "The Arcadeia." It is a designation that points as far back as the ancient Greek fantasy about the Golden Age that they located among the isolated Arcadian hills, where they imagined simple, happy shepherd boys and girls living (under the influence of the goat-footed rural god Pan) lives of "innocent" delight, piping and dancing as they desired and courted one another. Out of these ostensibly simple elements flowered

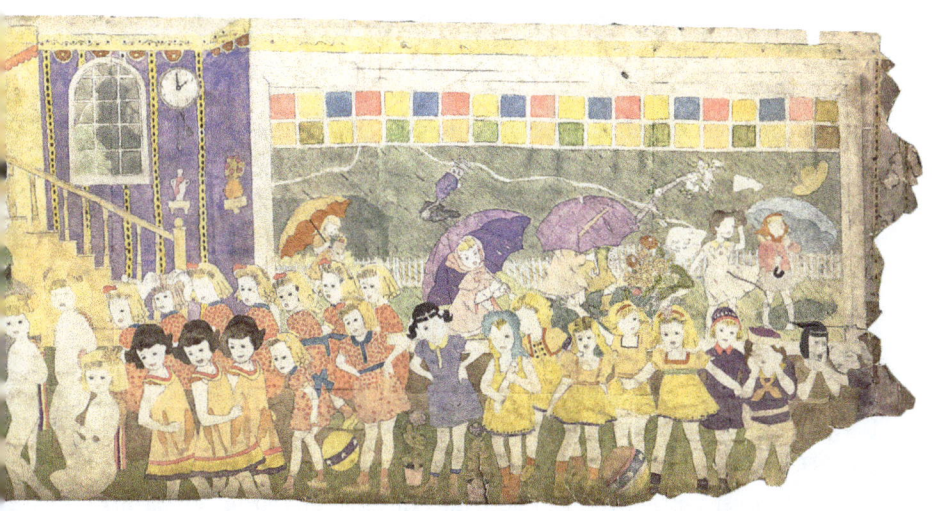

the tradition of the Arcadian romance, culminating (among other places) in Sir Philip Sidney's *Arcadia* (ca. 1578–84)—a kind of high Elizabethan "In the Realms of the Unreal"—and in Poussin's celebrated painting (1647) *Et in Arcadia Ego*, which depicts a small band of Golden Age shepherds contemplating the melancholy truth that death extends its reign even into their enviably happy homeland. Similarly, Darger's glowing, animated, beflowered interiors habitually open outward onto the destructive storms that lash the windows even of his "Arcadeias."

Darger's portmanteau term "Arcadeia" also points the viewer forward, to the distinctively modern space of the Arcade(s) in which Walter Benjamin located (and spent many years of his writing life composing "volutes" about) the emergence of modern urban space and its attendant realities and effects.[2] For Benjamin, Charles Baudelaire, through his poetry, served as Virgil to the modern *flâneur* who wandered the space of Paris's shopping arcades—covered but open, ambiguously inside outside, public but strangely intimate—from which both the twentieth-century shopping mall and the uncanny space of Darger's "Arcadeia" interiors are descended. Such visions of Darger's can be seen as way stations on an only partially chartable journey that we moderns take from "unreal" Arcadias to the unreal of the "real" arcades with which our worlds, including our digital worlds, are now honey-combed.

One other quite different emerging body of scholarship that deserves recognition and acknowledgment at the outset of a discussion of Darger and his resources is the new work on the effects in both the narrative and visual fields of the transference of work across media in the current digital age. Early news reports about Darger's writing habitually referred to his 15,000-page *In the Realms of the Unreal* as "the world's longest novel," despite the fact that the work arguably does not correspond to even the loosest notion of what a novel may be. Children's serial fiction—from Horatio Alger to *The Bobbsey Twins*, Nancy Drew, and beyond, which peaked in popularity during Darger's childhood and early adulthood—is one obvious model (along with the US Civil War chronicle, and ongoing newspaper accounts of subsequent wars) for Darger's main writing project, but other long and virtually interminable forms of visual-and-verbal narrative such as the videogame offer other, possibly more illuminating, models of what Darger was up to than that of writing and illustrating a novel. The various contributors to Pat Harrigan and Noah Wardrip-Fruin's edited volume, *Third Person: Authoring and Exploring Vast Narratives*, range in their focus from television serials (*Doctor Who*, *The Wire*) to role-playing games and board war games and popular book series in fantasy and science fiction. The length and scope of Darger's projects seem much less anomalous when viewed in such contexts. Happily, Michael Bonesteel, who (along with John M. MacGregor) had already done so much early on to enable the study of Darger's life and of the relation of his work to popular sources, has contributed a chapter to this pioneering collection, "Henry Darger's Search for the Grail in the Guise of a Celestial Child."

In fundamental consonance with the kinds of claims that are now beginning to be made on behalf of Darger's work—that it possesses "classic" elements that extend back across more than two millennia, and that it bears a family resemblance to the latest modes of digital visual narrative and their closest cognate forms—*Darger's Resources* proposes to extend the explorations that others have begun of Darger's extensive participation in and contribution to the mass culture of his century.

Contemplating the "outsider artist" Henry Darger (1892–1973), we begin with the myth of a life and career that is in some ways already deep-rooted, despite his having become the focus of much public attention only in the past ten years or so. The myth holds that Darger produced his work in something approaching absolute isolation, never showing it to anyone else, laboring over it continuously for sixty completely solitary years, coming home from his job as a janitor and writing and painting through the evening, perhaps far into the night, with nary a response from anyone else. Even in comparison with the lives of other so-called outsider artists and writers, Darger's sounds as though it may have been the loneliest ever.

This book has been written to try to help dispel that myth. This is not to deny that Darger led an outwardly solitary existence, nor that he seems to have succeeded in keeping his literary and artistic work to himself. It is, rather, to insist that although he appears to have strenuously avoided contact with his neighbors and fellow workers, he fashioned a populous other world for himself, in which he could live out a virtual existence replete with both the intense excitement and the lively sociability that seems so conspicuously missing from his allegedly real life.

Although the bare outlines of Darger's situation may look almost like a parody of the Romantic idea of the solitary, isolated, tragically misunderstood artist, his work, when one studies it, reveals itself as having been highly relational and even in some ways collaborative. One thing about which almost everyone who has reflected on Darger's work agrees is that it is appropriative in the extreme: he traced the figures that appear in his art out of coloring books, comic strips, newspapers, and magazines, and he collaged into his drawings images as diverse as Roman Catholic holy-card depictions of the Sacred Heart of Jesus, the little Coppertone girl having her swimsuit bottom pulled partway down by a playful cocker spaniel, and a celebrated landscape painting of an ominous "calm before the storm" (a theme dear to Darger) by the nineteenth-century artist Martin Johnson Heade. Similarly, in his 15,000-page-long *The Story of the Vivian Girls in What Is Known as the Realms of the Unreal, of the Glandeco-Angelinian War Storm, Caused by the Child Slave Rebellion*, he sometimes reproduces entire chapters, with only occasional changes of names and wording, from books as varied as John Bunyan's *Pilgrim's Progress* and James Oliver Curwood's *The Flaming Forest*, a 1920s male adventure and romance novel about Mounties fighting fires in the wilds of Canada. Darger not only "borrows" characters and situations from novels, histories, pious devotional works, newspaper comic strips, and children's serial books (*The Wizard of Oz, Heidi, The Bobbsey Twins, The Banner Boy Scouts*, and the sequels to all of these), at times juxtaposing Mutt and Jeff with Harriet Beecher Stowe's Little Eva or Charles Dickens's Fagin and Bill Sykes.

Far from living in some kind of historical and cultural vacuum, Darger in his extremely productive—albeit invisible to his contemporaries—career as a writer and artist enacted and embodied a new set of possibilities for a member of his proletarian class, living as a working adult outside any family structure. Darger was literate in a highly absorptive way but also in a highly productive way—unlike most omnivorous readers, he probably wrote even more than he read. He may have received some elementary (but, given his talent, extremely stimulating and valuable) training in watercolor painting in the institution where he spent his adolescence. Learning to read as he may well have done from the blazing color pages of the Sunday comics (he and the Sunday comics were born the same year), Darger also grew up with the movies and an unprecedented tide of popular and cheap print—the illustrated children's books, devotional pamphlets and prayer cards, and pulp magazines that, taken together, offer the closest analogues to the kinds of material Darger wrote, drew, and painted. In retrospect, we can see him as, in his way, a heroic and inspired cultural worker participating (as many of his contemporaries were) in an emerging proletarian public sphere that flourished for a few decades early in the twentieth century. Come the end of the Great Depression and the Second World War, parts of that sphere vanished as if overnight and other parts of it went underground—but its traces are still numerous and obvious to those interested in seeing them, and still alluring to the many of us who remain fascinated with projects of recovering the lost histories of the freaks, perverts, alleged crazies, and radical do-it-yourselfers—some working in bands, others toiling away alone in their little rooms—who produced much of the most vital culture of the past century.[1]

There is a story, in many ways upbeat, to be told about some of the splendid successes of early twentieth-century proletarian culture, such as the great musical and dance styles of jazz and blues that first emerged from the taverns, juke joints, and bordellos of New Orleans and the Mississippi Delta, Kansas City, and Chicago. But there is a somewhat more melancholy—and in some ways, perhaps, disturbing—set of stories to be told about the widespread, although far from total, defeat of the proletarian culture of the earlier decades of Darger's life. Darger shared with many of his contemporaries a strong affinity for lost causes—not the proverbial Lost Cause of the Confederacy after the Civil War, but what many experienced by the end of the 1930s as the larger lost cause of US service or menial workers and working-class women and children. In the Realms of the Unreal in one sense presents a far-from-perfect utopia or heaven in which Darger imagines other innocent and deeply oppressed people like himself finding some measure of salvation, or at least intermittent relief from suffering and social death. Perhaps the most challenging aspect of Darger's work lies in the way that he continually interweaves his visions of a proletarian utopia with his no less intense visions of the communicating hells of the range of experiences of violence and violation to which the members of the US proletariat of his time were disproportionately vulnerable. From the otherwise incoherently broad array of his sources and resources, Darger fashions over the first seven decades of the twentieth century an extraordinarily full elaboration of the pain and despair, but also hope and pleasure, that he experienced in his own life and that he imagined others feeling who occupied similar cosmic niches in the realms of the real and unreal.[2]

What if we see each of Darger's innumerable borrowings as a kind of invitation to other artists and writers and readers to be part of his virtually endless project of "translating" the books and images he collected in his room and in his mind into "the realms" he invented and inhabited in his imagination? Darger's painting and writing are routinely called his "work," but in an important sense Darger's work was scrubbing floors and doing laundry in a series of large hospitals (I like to think that he may have gotten really good after awhile at spending more and more time in the Realms with the Vivian Girls and their other friends even as he did his job).

Darger's art and writing may also have been his "work" in some sense, but they were also his play and his pleasure—or so I have preferred to take them. But of course "work" and "play" are hardly watertight, mutually exclusive categories. Studying Darger's writing and drawing during the past decade, I have often been forcefully reminded that beyond an initial point, play isn't simply fun, and neither are the intenser reaches of pleasure. The seriousness (as well as the great energy and joy) that children sometimes bring to their play can be, to anyone who is mindful of it, all the reminder one needs that play and pleasure—which in our society frequently get relegated to the domain of an ostensibly temporary escape from reality—both can demand engagement with some of our own and other people's most disturbing feelings, memories, and desires, and can invite and withstand rigorous analysis. What I have attempted to do in the following pages is to explore some of the possible bases on which one may, if one is so inclined, intensely enjoy Darger's writing and drawing while also attempting to come to some kind of terms with its often troubling relation to extreme violence, especially against little girls.

Students of Darger often wonder how he could have been as prolific and productive as he was, given the extreme solitude in which he worked. Indeed, in the absence of any apparent audience, however small, for his output, some critics seem to feel the need to posit something like a lifelong pathological compulsion on his part, some sort of virtual addiction to writing (hypergraphia) and drawing that compelled him to keep producing his work despite his isolation. Even in comparison with other artists famed for their reclusiveness—Emily Dickinson, say—Darger seems a remarkable case, for despite her apparent unwillingness to publish her poetry through the usual channels during her lifetime, Dickinson is known to have circulated her writing among an extensive circle of friends and literary advisors, and even to have allowed a handful of her poems to appear in print. Darger, as far as we know, hardly ever solicited the response of any other person to his work. The exception of which we are aware is his apparent involvement of his buddy William "Willie" Schloeder in the "child-protection league" of "the Gemini," which was an important focus of some of his writing and collage in the early stages of his career.[3] But what if, rather than assuming that there is something inherently tragic and deeply regrettable about Darger's apparent lack of an audience during his lifetime, we allow ourselves to entertain the possibility that he didn't show his work to other people because he didn't want or need to? What I continue to be struck by as I keep returning to his work is the particular kind of apparently infinitely renewable playfulness it exudes, one that is patently interactive, one that posits the active involvement of others in its narrative and pictorial gestures, despite (because of?) the outwardly solitary conditions under which he produced it.

Dissatisfied with his ability to draw the human figure, Darger initially experimented with collaging photographs of children and soldiers cut out of newspapers and magazines, embellishing them with his own drawing. For most of his career, he traced the images of the children he drew, scavenging them from print sources of several kinds, getting them photographically enlarged to fit into the large-scale panoramic visual style he developed, and organizing them into groups in landscapes of his own devising that were themselves collaged from elements clipped from newspapers and magazines. Students of his writing continue to discover in it an analogous practice of collaging language, character, and plot—sometimes just a name or a phrase, sometimes whole passages of other writers' prose.

Looking for the first time through the hundred or so books that Darger left in his room, I was intrigued to discover copies of *Pilgrim's Progress* and *Don Quixote*—not only two of the foundational texts for the formation of modern fictional narrative, but also each a book possessing the notable feature of usually appearing in tandem with its own sequel: *Don Quixote: Part One* (1605) and *Part Two* (1615), and *Pilgrim's Progress: The First Part* (1678) and *The Second Part* (1684). Given this, along with the high frequency of other serial works in his personal library—above all, his dozen or so volumes from the Oz series— it seems to me that it would be appropriate to say that Darger favored books (like his own) that "sequelate," that require and invite continuation beyond their initial would-be endings. Even Harriet Beecher Stowe's *Uncle Tom's Cabin*, the other title that must be mentioned along with the works of Cervantes and Bunyan (and the Oz series) in any account of the books most important to Darger and his work, has a distinguished place in the company of celebrated sequelating narratives. Although it spawned no literal sequel, *Uncle Tom's Cabin* did generate adaptations of itself in other media with remarkable energy and effect for decades after its appearance. Indeed, the film historian Linda Williams has argued that adaptations of Stowe's novel first transformed the history of the American theater (by bringing a particular brand of racialized melodrama into its foreground), and then, a generation later, similarly transformed the history of early American film (in uneasy tandem with D. W. Griffith's *Birth of a Nation*, perhaps the most powerful of counter-*Tom* texts, which rendered abject the kind of characters that Stowe had made heroic, and promoted the Ku Klux Klan as the hope of the nation).[4]

Darger's apparently strong attraction to *Uncle Tom's Cabin*—he frequently includes in his work samples of its language, characters, and plot—is particularly interesting in relation to its capacity for producing transformative adaptations of itself across media and across the technologies of new media. As someone who devoted about three decades (from roughly 1908 to around 1938) to writing a vast narrative about pious little girls drawn into a war over slavery, and who then spent even more decades "sequelating" the work by illustrating it, Darger may well have felt some especially strong artistic and imaginative affinities with a work with the metamorphic performative energies across media that *Uncle Tom's Cabin* had proved to have.[5]

Narratives that continue unfolding indefinitely, beyond what have long been taken to be the usual signs of closure—a significant death, a marriage, the end of a protracted crisis such as a war—these are the kinds of writing and storytelling that many twentieth-century producers and consumers of narrative have appeared to enjoy most, Darger certainly among them.[6] Let's consider for a moment the few facts we know about his actual social life in relation to the model of social production and reproduction one might have picked from the types of series that dominated mass print (and later film) culture in its earlier forms. Darger is not known to have had more than one friend, the aforementioned William Schloeder. He and Darger befriended each other fairly early in their lives: two of the four extant photographs of Darger show him with Schloeder. Darger records in his autobiography some of his cherished memories of chasing fires around the city with "Willie" and of treating his buddy to rides and food at the local amusement park. The two remained friends for years and then corresponded after Schloeder moved away from Chicago in middle age.[7]

Darger wrote about himself and Schloeder as "the Gemini," the twins, and the two young men appear to have made some (unsuccessful) efforts to adopt a child. Darger appears to have discovered—possibly to his considerable dismay—in this process that his society had stringent and narrow conceptions of who was fit to adopt a child. The children's series and serialized fiction for adults to which Darger seems to have been devoted throughout his life might well have given him (and some of their millions of other readers) a notion of how people go about forming families that was rather different from the normative one of the male-female couple's progress through courtship, marriage, and home- and baby-making. Indeed, a lot of the erotic glamour and allure of serial fiction for both children and adults may have proceeded for many readers from the apparent ease and frequency with which characters in these narratives formed closely bound groups, packs, bands, or gangs and further increased their numbers by formally and informally adopting others (new friends, neighbors, sometimes even chance acquaintances) into these expansive and flexible social and emotional networks as virtual parents, offspring, or siblings. This is as true of the earlier kinds of boys' series that Darger read and collected—such as *The Banner Boy Scouts* and its sequels—as it is (as I shall discuss below) of the most popular newspaper comic strips of the 1920s and 1930s, where the rash of adoptions included Dick Tracy's, of a little detective son. Since the young Darger may have, in his own mind, fairly effortlessly invented "the Gemini," as he and Schloeder became friends, why shouldn't they, we can imagine him wondering—if popular serial narratives, comic strips, and so on were any indication of the way things really worked—just go on sequelating, into a small family of two young men and an infant or small child (or two or three)?

I have written elsewhere about how Horatio Alger's boy heroes form families by taking in a second boy, nursing their often shared nest eggs (modest savings) until they are socially and financially able to draw more struggling boys off the street into their hyperdomestic, downright "broody" households.[8] Along such lines, Alger had constructed one of the most influential and enduring series of boys' books from the end of the Civil War through the years of Darger's early childhood, going Benjamin Franklin several better by imbricating the habit of saving money (thrift) with the formation of idyllic, all-boy families. That's not how things worked out for Darger and Schloeder, and the mode in which Darger's work sequelates is quite different from that in which Alger's does. Apparently, as it became clear that Darger and Schloeder were not going to be allowed to adopt a child, the Gemini redefined themselves as a child-protection society. As far as we know, all the attempted and achieved child protecting they did would be done in Darger's subsequent writing and drawing, for *In the Realms of the Unreal* organizes itself around a seemingly endless series of bands of little girl rebels and warriors who are pursued, menaced, and captured, and then either escape, are rescued, or face martyrdom (Darger's beloved stars, the seven dazzling Vivian Girls, always survive).

Darger's characters (and characteristic narratives) sequelate not by forming new families of children, but by discovering at crucial moments in the saga that beloved friends are actually close kin, either of the Vivians or of their strongest allies in the war, the Aronburg sisters. Closely related to the narratives of adoption that cluster around the Vivian Girls are a number of related stories in which the girls eventually discover that a child ally who has come to them as a stranger is actually a secret sibling—sometimes at the same time that they discover that a longtime boy ally is actually a girl. The most spectacular example of this kind of narrative in Darger's work is that of James Radcliffe, the dashing Rattlesnake Boy and constant companion of Penrod, the main boy hero of In the Realms (who himself is ultimately revealed to be the Vivian Girls' long-lost little brother). Through many volumes of the narrative, Radcliffe is simply an ace boy scout and a champion boxer and wrestler, but at least a few times the narrator drops hints that suggest that young James may be even more interesting than he already appears to be ("there was something queer about Radcliffe").[9] Finally, it is revealed that the Rattlesnake Boy is not only a girl disguised as a boy, but is actually Anna Aronburg. She is the sister of Angelinia Aronburg, an "adopted Vivian sister" (along with the Vivian Girls, the most important of the leaders of the child slave rebellion), and of Annie Aronburg, a key leader in the early stages of the war. Annie's gruesome martyrdom at the hands of a band of Glandelinians, the ferociously sadistic enemy troops of Darger's saga (along with Darger's loss of a photograph of her), has highly mysterious but nevertheless enormous consequences for the fortunes of both sides in the war for thousands of pages afterward.[10]

The Rattlesnake Boy's sex change is not without precedent in mainstream American children's literature; a similar event occurs at a key moment in a book that Darger most likely knew well, L. Frank Baum's The Marvelous Land of Oz (1904), the first sequel to The Wonderful Wizard of Oz (1900). In it the boy hero, Tip, who turns out to be the heir to the throne, is a girl called Princess Ozma, who had been turned into a boy by the sorceress Mombi. In the culminating pages of the book, the boy Tip is changed back into Princess Ozma so that she can take her place as the rightful successor to her late father as ruler of Oz.[11] As various of Baum's essays and prefaces make clear, he saw himself as engaged in a career-long project of producing a distinctively modern brand of fairy tale, one in which traditional magic would alternate with the modern marvels of technology—emblematized by the various female monarchs (rescued princesses and good witches) who rule over Oz.[12] (These figures are a tribute to traditionally female fairy power as well as to modern feminism—along with Susan B. Anthony and Elizabeth Cady Stanton, Baum's mother-in-law, Matilda Joslyn Gage, was a leading first-generation American feminist author and organizer.) Oz's female rulers are complemented by the many heroic or mock-heroic male automata who support female rule at the same time that they protect and serve as companions to the child characters who bear much of the narrative burden of Baum's stories. He drew not only on traditional popular theater such as fairy pantomime for its climactic transformation — including gender-transformation — scenes, but also on the nascent musical-comedy practices of the early twentieth century, such as when lines of what are unmistakably chorus girls arrayed in kick lines ("General Jinjur" and her all-girl army) come marching and dancing their way onto the scene in *The Marvelous Land of Oz*. It is easy to see how Baum may have served an especially enabling role for Darger, who similarly enjoyed juxtaposing old-fashioned and newfangled styles, folk figures alongside mass-culture ones. In his paintings, chubby birds out of cartoons and coloring books light on branches as girl warriors troop by, or as girl martyrs solemnly await their fates.

Whether or not Darger was aware of the long tradition of Victorian fairy pantomime behind it, Tip's transformation into Ozma was a more immediate resource for his habit of drawing schematic little male genitals on his legions of (as he put it) "nuded" girl warriors. John MacGregor, who carried out much of the early exhaustive research on Darger's writing as well as his visual art, raises an interesting question about the change of gender of James Radcliffe/Anna Aronburg: if everyone in Darger's world has male genitals and no one has female ones, as his drawings suggest, what is it that is supposed to mark true gender in the bodies of the persons who inhabit the realms of the unreal?[13] The enduring scandal of Darger's work may be not that it endowed girls with diminutive male genitals, or that it showed some of its girl characters disemboweled or dismembered, but that being successfully "masculine" in Darger's world in the most obvious and unchallengeable ways (by being a champion athlete and a courageous soldier) is a role that can be played exceedingly well by a child, especially by a little girl.

In this dominant feature, Darger's work strikingly resembles not only the Victorian fairy spectacle, but also the extremely popular manga about the phallic warriorgirl that has recently spread from Japan to many other parts of the world. The prominent Japanese social psychologist Tamaki Saitō notes the similarity and devotes a chapter to Darger's work in his recent psychoanalytic study of the sexuality of *otaku* (obsessive fans of manga, anime, and related video games).[14] Saitō argues that the desire (erotic and otherwise) of the otaku is "to create an autonomous object of desire within the fictional space" of manga and anime — to develop real feelings of intense fondness and sexual attraction to "drawn characters" (classically, girl warrior ones).

Saitō finds a remarkable anticipation of this controversial form of desire in Darger's struggles to imbue his writings and drawings with "their own autonomous reality," one that could eventually render ordinary social and sexual satisfactions (or the lack thereof) irrelevant.[15]

Darger's involvement in sequelating forms and their effects is consequently quite different from Louisa May Alcott's, who famously wrote on the closing page of one of her long-running series that she fervently hoped a volcano might now engulf the land of *Little Women* — thus relieving her of the possibility that her publisher and all-too-faithful readers would force yet one more sequel from her weary pen. Her assumption might have seemed an incomprehensible one to Darger, whose work, far from being slowed down by the equivalent of an erupting volcano, appears actually to depend for its continuation on the recurrence of one massive disaster — fire, storm, or military conflagration — after another. Of course Darger, who received no money for his serial productions and supported his work as a writer and artist out of his meager earnings as a janitor, experienced different kinds of financial pressures than did successful children's authors like Alcott or Alger or Baum. Nonetheless, Darger appears to have continued to write and draw energetically and (as far as we can tell) pleasurably until very near the end of his long life.

Historians of popular literature of this period have tended to overemphasize economic and financial factors, almost to the exclusion of other likely motives among a given author's reasons for producing sequel after sequel to a particular work. One exception to this tendency is the Oz scholar Michael O. Riley, who maintains that Baum wrote the last several volumes that he contributed to the Oz series for much-needed money but also for love of what Oz had come to mean to him as a popular utopian myth of an America somehow purged of its chronic and catastrophic social and economic failures.[16] Much as he appears to have loved and imitated the Oz books, Darger never became such an idealizing patriot of the unfulfilled promise of the United States as Baum did, or as much of a utopian as Baum eventually was. Darger lacks both Baum's hope for the arrival of a nation-saving, matriarchal other America, and Alger's faith in the allegedly boy-saving, boy-loving, boy-bonding benefits of an early form of corporate capitalism. Darger's fantasy of saving or rescuing little girls from slavery, imprisonment, torture, or death — and (as MacGregor has suggested) ultimately of being himself adopted or otherwise conscripted into a dazzling gang of little girls like the Vivians — engenders a particularly unstable form of sequelation. Darger's work continues to oscillate all his life between sometimes horrifying scenes of children being massacred and their alternative, scenes of children in a pastoral setting, that even at their most idyllic show the next thunderstorm or cyclone moving inexorably toward the center of the picture. *In the Realms of the Unreal* consequently has two mutually exclusive possible—but never achieved—endings, one in which the Christian forces prevail, and another in which the Glandelinians, after pretending to officially surrender, march out to take up arms and instruments of torture against the child rebels all over again. MacGregor says that Darger stopped writing about war after he finished writing *In the Realms* in the late 1930s and subsequently wrote only about natural disasters,[17] but Darger did not stop painting scenes of war, including scenes of massacre and atrocity. Although *Further Adventures in Chicago: Crazy House*, the formal sequel to *In the Realms*, is not about war in the literal sense, it is about hauntedness, demonic possession, and horrific violence—truly a continuation of war by other means.

A volatile mode of sequelation also pervades the relation of the remarkable series of dozens of panoramic watercolor drawings that Darger produced, mostly in the second half of his adult life, to accompany the fifteen thousand pages of saga he had written in the first half. To date, most of the critical attention that has been paid to Darger and his work has focused on his paintings and, to a considerable degree, on reaching conclusions about the personal psychology that they allegedly reflect or imply. Since the most extensive and thoroughly researched early commentary on Darger and his work is that of MacGregor, who combines the study of outsider art with training and practice in clinical psychiatry, the first authoritative-sounding stories told about Darger tended to emphasize an isolating and pathologizing version of both the man and his art, from MacGregor's early pronouncements that Darger had been "psychologically . . . a serial killer" (albeit one who, MacGregor went on to say, "sublimated" his supposedly killer instincts "into his art") to MacGregor's later, more measured diagnosis of Asperger's syndrome.[18] My aim in this book has been to contribute to other ways of thinking about where the undeniable power of Darger's work comes from, ways that recognize the variety and intensity of the creative energies that he and his work derive from his lifelong involvement in the renaissance of vernacular writing and visual art that occurred in his world as the nineteenth century drew to its close and continued through the opening decades of the twentieth—a development to which we can now see Darger's work as constituting a remarkable addition.

A corollary aim of this book is to promote some recognition that Darger's tendency to return to scenes of massacre and atrocity, rather than simply being a symptom of personal psychological damage on his part, may be better understood as the expression of a profound fidelity to some important but generally unwelcome truths about the place of just such forms of extreme violence, often perpetrated against highly vulnerable populations, in the history of the development and expansion of the Americas down through Darger's own lifetime. To be fair to MacGregor, I want to acknowledge that he makes the point in his monograph on Darger that the artist somehow anticipates and registers in his work a number of the most terrible political realities of twentieth-century history, from the relegation of millions to enslavement and murder in the concentration camps of the Shoah to the atomic bombing of Hiroshima and Nagasaki.[19] MacGregor ascribes this to the uncanny vision that disturbed persons sometimes have. I would argue instead that Darger may have been able in a sense to foresee some of the most terrible episodes in the history of his time (including episodes that had not yet actually occurred) because as a member of one thoroughly marginalized group—the so-called feebleminded—he may have had a particularly strong awareness of and sensitivity to the long history of systemic violence that, explicitly and implicitly, had been used to try to subdue his own and other vulnerable populations, including the working poor, recent immigrants, African Americans, Native Americans, and feisty women and girls like the ones Darger champions and idealizes in his work. MacGregor and other writers have offhandedly called In the Realms of the Unreal "a novel," perhaps "the longest novel in existence." But "novel" hardly begins to answer the question of what manner of prose narrative In the Realms may be. It is, rather, a highly unusual kind of amalgam of the children's adventure serial with the war chronicle and the atrocity narrative, an ancient kind of writing that has (lamentably) become ubiquitous in modernity.[20]

For an example of the kinds of sequelation and collage in Darger's painting through which he explores both his often terrifying vision of political violence against the vulnerable and his often consoling sense of the virtual emotional and spiritual haven that various kinds of mass-culture narratives and images may afford them, let's look at what is in many ways a representative painting of Darger's, At Jennie Richee. While sending warning to their father watch night black cloud of coming storm thro' windows (ca. 1945) (fig. 4). The painting, which is about a foot and a half high and about six feet wide, depicts a scene said to be set at Jennie Richee, a battle site in the realms of the unreal where quite a high percentage of Darger's panorama paintings are set. Some of the scenes, such as this one, show safe and peaceful-looking interiors, but Jennie Richee is apparently not only or not always a domestic haven; a number of the paintings set there show outdoor scenes in which the Vivian Girls and their friends are escaping—to or from—Jennie Richee; it's not clear in some of the images which direction the escape is taking. Jennie Richee can sometimes be a place of detention, occupied by the Glandelinians, as in the painting, *At Jennie Richee. Arrested or Captured by the Enemy Again*.[21] Yet another painting set at Jennie Richee shows the Vivian Girls running to warn their father, the emperor, of impending trouble; it is unclear here whether Jennie Richee is where their father is or—as in the present image—a safe place from which they can send him a message.[22]

Darger drew and painted this picture (as he did many of his large paintings) on three large pieces of paper glued together with homemade flour-and-water paste. The composition divides fairly precisely in half along a vertical axis in the very center. On the right-hand side, a group of nine children (eight girls and a boy) and one adult male stand before two sets of large double windows through which we can see bursts of lightning playing. We know the two adult male soldiers here are benign because their uniforms are purple and yellow, the colors of the good-guy forces (three of the girls in the picture wear purple as well). At each of the two double windows, a couple of children appear to be absorbed in watching the lightning. Two of the other girls in the scene appear to be interacting with the adult male—is it the Vivian Girls' guardian, Captain Jack Evans?—and two of the girls and the boy face toward the viewer. On the left-hand side of the painting, another military officer stands, apparently accepting a written message to be conveyed to the emperor—or he may be seeing off one of the older Vivian sisters, who, unlike the other nine children in the picture, is dressed for travel in a coat, carrying a purse and gloves, and who may be going to deliver the message to her father in person.

The adult males and children in the scene are typical of such figures across the entire range of Darger's visual work, traced as they all are from various source materials collected by the artist and bearing the traces in several instances of having been produced in the first place for the purpose of modeling a uniform or children's "fashion." What is unusual, even perhaps unique, about this particular painting of Darger's is the inclusion in the third, left-hand window—the one through which no one in the image is looking—of a color reproduction of an oil painting by another artist, Martin

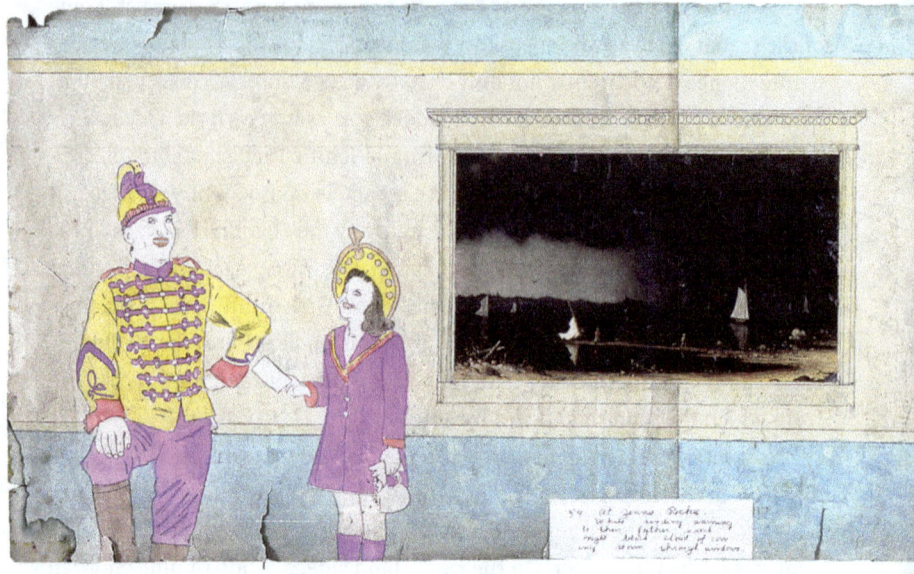

FIGURE 4. Henry Darger. *At Jennie Richee. While sending warning to their father watch night black cloud of coming storm thro' windows.* Copyright Kiyoko Lerner, courtesy of Andrew Edlin Gallery.

Johnson Heade's celebrated 1868 work, *Thunderstorm on Narragansett Bay*. As a highly dramatic visual depiction of an ominously blackening sky reflected in a body of water, the image must have appealed strongly to Darger's fascination with the suspenseful moment of calm that precedes the unleashing of a powerful, potentially destructive storm. It is a fascination that Heade shared; he produced a now-famous series of paintings of such scenes. Heade was a bit of an outsider artist himself. He had served a close apprenticeship with Edward Hicks, who painted the Peaceable Kingdom series, perhaps the most highly iconic image in the American folk-art tradition. As a young man, Heade had practiced what was even at that time the rapidly disappearing occupation of itinerant portrait painter. Although he subsequently lived and painted in New York City and socialized and shared work space with some of the most successful painters of the time, Heade was generally not taken up by art patrons or the press. Many viewers, including professional ones, were puzzled or put off by his series of inky-black storm scenes, as they were by his later series of hummingbirds with orchids and other exotic blossoms, all painted with a kind of hypnotic attention and with recognizably intense

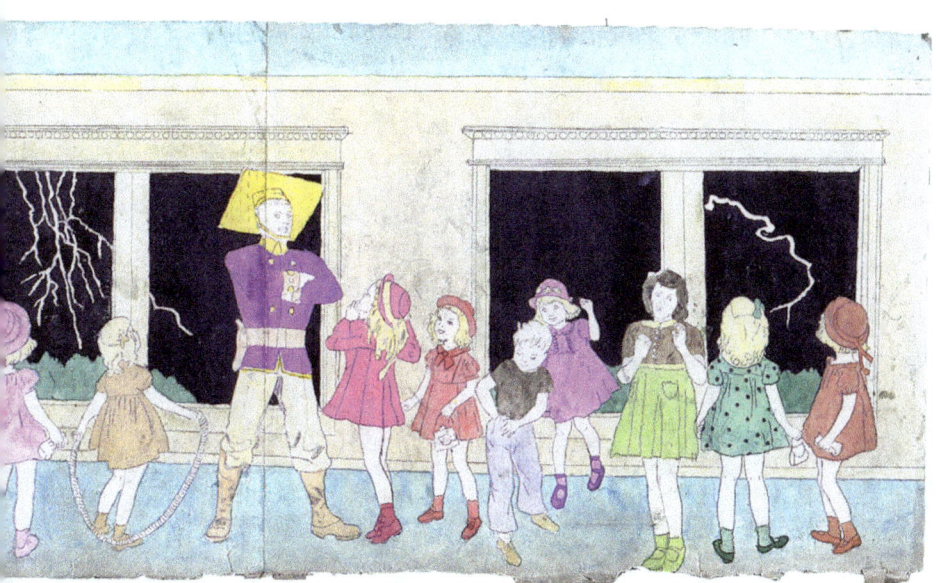

erotic pleasure of some not readily definable kind (Darger wittingly or un-wittingly recognized a brother artist when he saw one).

Michael Bonesteel tells us that this is the only instance of Darger's work-ing a high-art image into one of his own paintings, and that Darger had come across the reproduction of Heade's painting in the February 1945 issue of the *Ladies' Home Journal*.[23] Heade's work had been generally forgotten after his death in 1904, until a sharp-eyed collector noticed *Thunderstorm on Nar-ragansett Bay* in a Larchmont antique store in 1941. The art world's response to Heade's work soon thereafter proved itself all that (perhaps more than) Heade could have desired; *Thunderstorm* was the widely publicized showpiece in an important exhibition of American Romantic painting at the Museum of Modern Art only a couple of years after its rediscovery. In Darger's paint-ing, the left-hand window serves as a frame for Heade's scene, which shows sailboats presumably heading for shore as the surface of the water on which they move appears to have become saturated with the darkness of the threat-ening sky. Sanford Schwartz has commented that whether Heade's paintings show a hummingbird poised before a much larger, frilly orchid or a few small

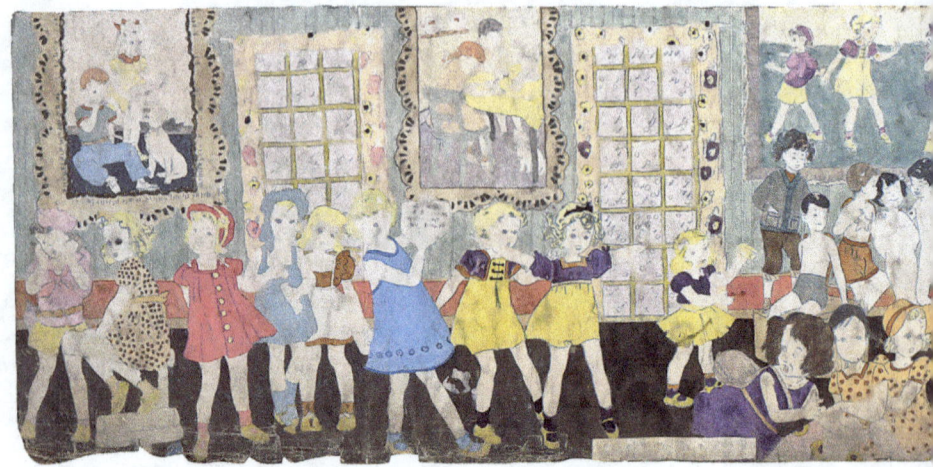

FIGURE 5. Henry Darger. *Untitled* ("*Part 2 of 205*"). Copyright Kiyoko Lerner, courtesy of Andrew Edlin Gallery.

vessels quietly getting out of the way of a potentially massive storm, "his best pictures are often about a standoff between the dire and the unfazed."[24]

Even in some of the most horrific scenes that Darger produced—including another one set at Jennie Richee, *At Jennie Richee again escape*—the Vivian Girls can appear unfazed even as they flee the dire scene of mass child crucifixion just behind them.[25] Perhaps in such images their behavior bespeaks a wish that at least some of the vulnerable persons in a given scene of violence and cruelty will be able to escape and survive even such terrible events. In probably the most horrific of all Darger's paintings, the triptych *They were almost murdered themselves*, which depicts scenes of torture and mutilation in wintry forests *At Norma Catherine via Jennee Richee* and also *At Jennee Richee via Norma*, however, the Vivian Girls appear vulnerable and even anguished as they struggle for their own lives against their would-be executioners.[26] Darger captions the right-hand painting of the triptych "Vivian Girl Princesses are forced to witness frightful murder massacre of children—Vivian Girls not shown in this composition." (A similar painting, in which they are absent from the frightful scene, *At Jullo Callio via Norma. From windows Vivian Girls witness harrowing and blood-curdling scenes*, shows them appearing distressed as they look out windows that reveal nothing to the viewer but large patches of bright blue sky.)[27] In many such images, Darger presses far beyond the

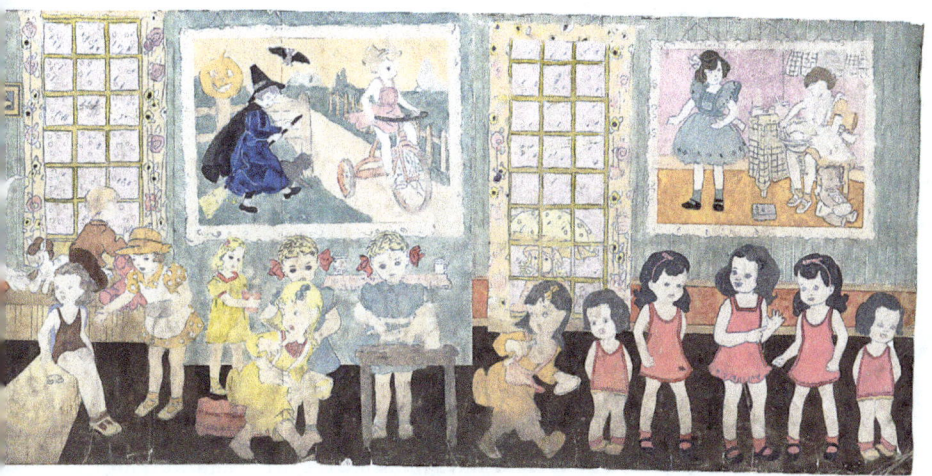

kind of "standoff between the dire and the unfazed" that impels some of his other, less overtly violent images, such as the several in which child characters find at least temporary shelter from the storm—At Jennie Richee. While sending warning is a typical example.

Although this image may be the only one into which Darger collages a reproduction of an entire painting by a high-art painter, it is only one among many in which he features other works of art, actual or imaginary. For example, Untitled ("Part 2 of 205") (fig. 5) appears to be set in the same kind of long, corridor-like room with three or four large windows across the rear of the image that we have just seen in At Jennie Richee. While sending warning and saw in the preface in Darger's Arcadeia painting. Untitled ("Part 2 of 205"), like many such interiors of Darger's, is crowded with a jumble of children clustered into various groups and guarded by a Blengin attendant, all in a setting decorated with large framed paintings-within-the-painting of children engaging in peaceful and playful activities—riding a tricycle, eating breakfast, or posing with their dog. A heavy rain or a mixture of rain and snow pelts the four large windows, and one little girl with umbrella walking through the storm past the right-most window is the sole outsider in what would otherwise appear to be an utterly safe space—were not another little girl (the sixth from the left) holding up a sign that says, "Don't worry we Blengins will help you escape." Escape from where? Possibly the cozy-looking, child-filled space we are beholding? Is it some kind of prison rather than a shelter, possibly a large and cheerfully furnished holding cell for another yet-to-be-staged Massacre of the Innocents? Or have the children now playing in the picture escaped from massacre (at least this time) to find (at least tempo-rary) shelter in this cozy interior with its flowery curtains? As is the case with so many of Darger's paintings, how can one be sure of the difference?

In a number of Darger's other paintings, the Christian armies decorate their interior spaces with such familiar Roman Catholic devotional images as the Sacred Heart, the Virgin Mary, and St. Teresa of Lisieux (known as the Little Flower). Darger traced some of these from printed images; for others, he collaged the printed source images directly into the picture. Predictably, when the Vivian Girls and their child allies infiltrate the living and working spaces of their enemies the Glandelinians, they find (but characteristically seem unfazed by) similarly monumentally large and imposing images—in these cases, life-size sculptures as well as two-dimensional depictions— of adult Glandelinian males strangling little girls. Each of the three largest populations in In the Realms—the "good" Angelinian or Abbieannian sol-diers, the "bad" Glandelinians, and the child rebels—are shown living among images that show them as they appear to themselves: the Catho-lic armies display large and numerous icons of their supernatural patrons, while the Glandelinians repose amid paintings and sculptures of themselves wreaking mayhem on children at those times when they are not actually out doing so, and a girl in a scene of idyllic child domesticity puts up curtains standing before a painting of another girl hanging out laundry.

MacGregor argues that we should regard Darger's production of visual work not so much as a making of paintings for others to view, but rather as a construction of environments for himself, in which he could, as it were, hang out with the Vivian Girls he loved and, in some sense, desired (and by whom he may have dreamed of being loved and desired). To this way of thinking, Darger's real existence was his "imaginary" one, and he produced first his writings and then his paintings to enable and support his relocation of his "real" life into "the realms of the unreal."[28] Although I have a lot of sympathy with and interest in this claim, I would also offer a different per-spective or epistemology about the function—for him, but potentially also for us—of Darger's inclusion of so many pictures-within-pictures. Even the most appealing and attractive environments, virtual or not, cannot be and perhaps need not be more than half-real. Certain stories or pictures can (sometimes) serve (at least some of) us as alternative environments, places we may come to inhabit with more pleasure and satisfaction than we can inhabit our actual lives. I believe that Darger's paintings also suggest that such environments are, ultimately, also only pictures—transitory, ephemeral, providing only temporarily the illusion (welcome as it may be) of another, better, happier, more pleasurable, and less violent and unpredictable world.[29]

One aspect of Darger's work that interpretations like MacGregor's—which see it as essentially a wish-fulfilling alternative environment or alternative reality—tend not to consider is Darger's way of carefully and precisely captioning his paintings, often with extensive notation of where the scene occurs and what is happening in it. If the images were designed to function only as psychic getaways and virtual playgrounds for the artist, I do not believe they would so often and so prominently feature paintings and other works of art within them, or include the often lengthy caption panels with which Darger has endowed so many of his pictures. Previous critics have interpreted the captions as forms of address that imply viewers and possibly a posterity for Darger's paintings (analogous to the frequent explicit addresses to readers in his writing). To this interpretation of Darger's captions as forms of address, I would add that the captions are also moments in which the images reflexively assert their status as objects of potential critical and self-critical awareness. They function in the same way that the many paintings-within-paintings and pictures-within-pictures in Darger's visual work do, as sites and moments of transition between mistaking a given painting or passage of his writing for something (or some place) entirely real or entirely unreal. As I shall discuss again later in the book, there are points in Darger's writing at which he not only includes himself as a character, but when he has other characters describe and discuss his behavior and opine that "he [Darger] must be some kind of nut." Darger's apparent ability to recognize, and his willingness to acknowledge, that at least some other people may find him or at least some of his behavior strange and even crazy bespeaks a lucid self-awareness that seems to me to belie any assumption that his work is best understood as solely a means of escape for him from social oppression or psychic pain.

Turning to Darger's resources as a primary focus for understanding his work is a move I have made precisely to try to counter the kinds of analyses that tend to regard Darger largely as a pitiful character who escaped his miserable existence by allowing himself (or feeling compelled) to be consumed with the project of producing an exorbitantly idiosyncratic record of his personal anguish. The more we study his work, the more we see, I think, that he was also a producer of a large body of aesthetically, affectively, and cognitively rich material, in the consideration of which there is much to enjoy as well as much to think about. Rather than seeing his work as providing us a window into a deeply disturbed psyche, we can take it as a series of views of many of the successes and pleasures of twentieth-century mass culture, as well as of the massive and recurrent racial, ethnic, and sexual violence perpetrated during the same period. Rather than condescendingly and misguidedly treating Darger only as a case study, we can look to his work for what it may tell us about both the powerful allure of mass-mediated narrative and imagery and the possibility (or impossibility) of escaping the labyrinthine and often terrifying histories and politics of which we in the world today are the direct heirs.

To recap: my main objective in this project has been to suggest some ways of regarding Henry Darger's work that deemphasize the alleged personal pathology that has provided most of the main terms of analysis in such influential early accounts of the man and his work as John MacGregor's, and to emphasize Darger's virtuosic recasting in his work of a remarkably broad range of graphic and print figures and narratives. I have also wanted to counter a tendency in writing about Darger and about twentieth-century outsider artists in general to assume that they were fundamentally without intellectual resources—an assumption I began questioning as soon as I discovered such volumes as *Don Quixote* and Anatole France's *Revolt of the Angels* among the books that Darger left in his room at the end of his life, or saw him citing in his writing the philosopher William James on the generally constructive and cooperative behavior of the alleged victims of natural disasters. Furthermore, I have wanted to try to work through some ways in which the mass culture of the twentieth century—pulp magazines, comic strips, children's book series—can also be understood as offering cognitive and intellectual, as well as aesthetic, resources to an absorptive and imaginative reader such as Darger. I have sought to counter what has struck me as an overinvestment on the part of many who have written about Darger in highlighting the supposedly extremely private quality of his existence in favor of seeing him as an active, enthusiastic, and highly productive participant in a rowdy and gaudy proletarian public sphere that waxed and waned during his long life. As I argue in some of the following pages, there are traces of such a public sphere in the anarchic and hooliganish comics of the early color supplements of the Sunday newspapers and in the weird and lurid covers of the pulp magazines. And against the trend of seeing Darger's work as manifesting either the mind of a serial killer—and a pedophile one at that—or nothing more than the stereotype of the weird but harmless (indeed, perhaps even innocent) man who wanders and mumbles about the neighborhood, rummaging through garbage cans and muttering comments about the weather to no one in particular, I have attempted to imagine a range of sexualities that could be associated with Darger's writing and drawing that are not very highly object-driven, but more inclined to the intense enjoyment of certain atmospheres, both spatial and narrative, than such more normatively adult sexual pleasures as penetration, consummation, and climax.

Readers relatively new to the study of Darger may be wondering where they can read his writing and see his paintings. Nearly three hundred watercolor and collage paintings by Darger are extant. Various paintings are now in the permanent collections of art museums around the United States (the Musée de l'Art Brut in Lausanne, Switzerland, also exhibits an important collection of Darger's paintings), and there have been major exhibitions in several US cities as well as in London, Paris, Berlin, and Tokyo. As part of its acquisition of Darger materials from Kiyoko Lerner in 2000, the Henry Darger Study Center at the American Folk Art Museum, in New York City, acquired more than two dozen of the large double-sided scroll paintings as well as several hundred of his smaller collages and pen or pencil study sketches. At the same time, the museum made itself the repository of virtually all of Darger's extant writings, including the fifteen-thousand-page *Story of the Vivian Girls, in What Is Known as the Realms of the Unreal* and its sequel, *Further Adventures in Chicago: Crazy House*, the five thousand pages of Darger's *History of My Life* (only the first two hundred pages of which are in any ordinary sense of the term autobiographical; the remaining thousands of pages chronicle the depredations of a huge tornado named "Sweetie Pie"), and six volumes of his weather journals.

Many images of Darger's paintings are available online; the extensive image gallery on the American Folk Art Museum's website is a good place to start. So far, only a tiny fraction of the vast store of Darger's writing has become available to readers. Bonesteel has provided an extensive sampling of it in print in the volume he edited, *Henry Darger: Art and Selected Writings*. MacGregor quotes Darger's writing copiously in *Henry Darger: In the Realms of the Unreal*, bringing together passages, many substantial in length, from something like the full range of the various writings. A thematic selection of excerpts titled "Thunderstorms and Atrocities: Excerpts from the Writings of Henry Darger" appears in Klaus Biesenbach's catalogue *Henry Darger: Disasters of War*, 193–205, which also includes sixty-six pages (printed in facsimile) of Darger's *History of My Life*, with a brief but stimulating introduction by Carl Watson. Despite the commendable efforts of all these scholars, only a tiny fraction of Darger's writing is available at present, except by visiting the American Folk Art Museum and consulting the manuscripts, which are in very fragile shape, or the microfilms of them, which are as variable in their legibility and reproducibility as microfilms tend to be.

Darger's former landlords, Nathan and Kiyoko Lerner, began acting not only to preserve his work but also to make it available to interested scholars and curators within a few years of his death. According to the cultural historian Ron Sakolsky, members of the Chicago Surrealist Group were among the first dozen or so people to be shown Darger's work and were the first to exhibit any of it anywhere—in an exhibition organized by the group titled "Surrealism in 1977" in Gary, Indiana.[30] There was another exhibition of Darger's work the same year, at the Hyde Park Art Center, in Chicago. Darger's reputation grew slowly for about twenty years after that, remaining a fairly resolutely underground one until the waves of publicity about him and his work that attended the opening of "The Unreality of Being," the American Folk Art Museum's exhibition of his work in New York City in 1997 (the show had originated at the University of Iowa Museum the year before, curated by Stephen Prokopoff). A second large wave of publicity ensued when the American Folk Art Museum announced its acquisition of its collection of Darger's work in 2000 and its opening of the Henry Darger Study Center. These events and the media coverage of them inaugurated Darger's career as a cult artist and a byword among urban hipsters for weird, kinky, excessive, faux-naïf do-it-yourself art. Darger's standing as "indy" icon began to coalesce with his reputation in the arts-and-performance mainstream in the first decade of the twenty-first century, with the publications of Bonesteel's, MacGregor's, and other lavishly produced and illustrated monographs on his work, and the ongoing transfiguration of his art and writing into poetry (by the likes of John Ashbery and Clayton Eshleman), pop music (Natalie Merchant and Sufjan Stevens), experimental theater (Mac Wellman and Ridge Theater), modern dance (Pat Graney and her company), and more art (for example, the 2008 Dargerism exhibition of new and recent work influenced by Darger, curated by Brooke Davis Anderson at the American Folk Art Museum).

Apropos of Darger's art in what Walter Benjamin called "the age of mechanical reproduction": almost without exception, the numerous reproductions of Darger's paintings that have appeared in the several large monographs that have been published are of excellent quality. Nevertheless, there are at least a couple of features of the work that, to my mind (and eye), reproductions tend not to capture adequately: the delicacy of Darger's drawing and the exquisite design of his enormous pictorial compositions, and I mean exquisite with respect to both his deployment of line and his application of color. It was these particular qualities of his work that powerfully drew me to it the first time I had a chance to see a lot of it at the 1997 American Folk Art Museum exhibition, and they have kept me strongly attached to it ever since—they and his obviously enduring affection for and enjoyment of comic strips, "holy cards," saints' legends, and children's chapter books.

Chapter 1

DARGER'S BOOK OF MARTYRS

> There is much to say about the fact that it is
> little girls who open themselves to this game
> and these hostilities. . . . Empirical violence,
> war in the colloquial sense (ruse and perfidy
> of little girls, *apparent* ruse and perfidy of little
> girls. . . .
> —Jacques Derrida, "The Violence of the
> Letter"

Henry Darger's fascination with pious stories about the torture and execution of angelic little girls—strangled, disemboweled, or crucified—may
seem remote from most people's experience nowadays. Yet I, born sixty years
after Darger, grew up in the 1950s in an environment similarly saturated with
the bloody and extreme, if highly stylized, violence of Roman martyr theater,
still considered at the time of my early education—at a parochial school in
a small Oklahoma town, staffed by members of the Felician Sisters order of
Lodi, New Jersey—to be an obvious source of edification for tender Catholic sprouts. Ancient adherents of the cult of Adonis, who celebrated by re-
enacting his fatal goring by the boar and his glorious rebirth each spring,
had nothing on us Catholic schoolchildren a couple of millennia later who,
under the nuns' tutelage and the gazes of our doting parents, celebrated
the end of the academic year each May by performing a Roman martyr play.
Imagine my excitement as a kindergartener when I was cast as the pagan
idol to whom young Saint Agnes (played by the most glamorous girl in the
eighth grade) would righteously refuse to offer incense! An untimely case of
the measles did me out of my chance (never to be offered again) to wear a
tiny toga and sandals and stand perfectly still on a pedestal during this tense

encounter between Agnes and the cruel emperor. To my deep disappointment, I got no role at all in the following year's martyr play, only to be cast as a singing and dancing teapot in a babyish musical number.

A few years later I remember our third- or fourth-grade class reading and discussing a rendition of the martyrdom of Saint Agnes in the Catholic comic-book *Treasure Chest* that we received at school. The comic's main ongoing feature, titled *This Godless Communism*, is available in its entirety on the Internet.[1] Although the publication promoted itself as a wholesome and even godly alternative to the trashy stuff we were supposedly reading at home (the favorite comics of my siblings and me were *Donald Duck* and *Classics Illustrated*, but such preferences may have been far from typical), it employed some of the same artists who produced the most sensational and (in some quarters) reviled comics of the time, including E. C. Comics' *Tales from the Crypt*. In scenes depicting the tortures the girl Agnes underwent for refusing to abandon her Christian faith, we children may well have found *Treasure Chest* more macabre, grotesque, and frightening than the ordinary green-ghoul fare our guardians worried about our consuming.

But in spite—or because—of its undeniable scariness, the legend of the martyrdom of Saint Agnes fascinated some of us children. I recall our being less taken with the next year's all-school play, *The Martyrdom of Saint Tarsicius*, the story of a pious Roman boy who allowed a mob of pagan males to beat him to death rather than give them the ciborium containing consecrated hosts that he was conveying to an underground cell of his fellow Christians. Given that the new plot was as weird and violent as the previous year's, our failure to embrace Saint Tarsicius's story as our own suggests that there were other factors in play for us than the story's high proportion of religious sadomasochism. I wonder if we might have been reacting to the insidious word "sissy" in this martyr's name. Even without the lexical nudge, it might have been hard for us not to feel that there was something sissyish (we didn't yet know the word "priggish") about Tarsicius's unyielding piety—as well as about his death at the hands of a mob of bullies. (Proper martyrs were burned, beheaded, or thrown to wild beasts, not bullied to death—a fate that struck far too close to the school playground.) So much of childhood bravado and self-respect depends on at least sometimes disobeying one's mother's orders not to allow oneself to be waylaid in the performance of one's errands that it may have been hard for us not to see Tarsicius's story as one that had been chosen to please not us, but the mothers and nuns who were our taskmasters.

The Second Vatican Council, which took place around the time I was finishing parochial school, worked its transformation on the church even in places like rural Oklahoma, making our youthful conscription as actors in grim and gruesome dramas of martyrdom seem almost unbelievably antediluvian. Only a handful of years, after all, separated our childhood performances as cruel emperors, pagan idols, and virgin martyrs from our early-adolescent renditions of Bob Dylan's "Blowin' in the Wind" and the Byrds' "Turn, Turn, Turn" at guitar masses. In those later years I occasionally wondered where our teachers had procured the scripts for those grade-school martyr pageants.

These little dramas were evidently a tributary of the torrent of mass-produced and mass-distributed Catholic devotional art—illustrated books, painted plaster statues for churches and homes, rosaries, holy cards bearing the images of Jesus and the saints, bottles of holy water, crucifixes, religious jewelry, medals, and scapulars—that began in the middle of the nineteenth century to be sold in dozens of shops in the immediate neighborhood of the Church of Saint Sulpice in Paris, still, albeit on a somewhat reduced scale, a center for the sale of such objects today. Rather than continuing to import these items from France, purveyors of "religious goods" in the United States began to produce and market their own versions around 1865; Barclay Street in lower Manhattan became "the American Saint Sulpice." The cultural historian Colleen McDannell writes: "By the end of the nineteenth century, l'art Saint-Sulpice became the international style of Catholic church art. From Ireland to Mexico to India to the United States, local art was replaced by goods either imported from France or copied from French standards."[2] But, she observes, well before then the denizens of both Saint Sulpice and Barclay Street had come under sustained attack for the alleged vulgarity and false piety (evident in the term "plaster saint") of the styles they purveyed—for their dissemination of what would come to be known as Catholic kitsch. The controversy between alleged sentimentalists and avowed modernists raged on for over half a century, until the Vatican itself undertook to criticize l'art Saint-Sulpice and its imitators around 1950 (171).

But even official disapproval from the highest place in the church could not immediately undo the fact that, as McDannell puts it, "for at least a hundred years, from 1840 to 1940, Catholic devotionalism and l'art Saint-Sulpice were closely aligned" (167). In response to the revolutionary and republican politics that had reemerged in every European generation since 1789, the church had in the late nineteenth century and the early twentieth sponsored a massive proliferation of new and revived Catholic devotional cults and paraliturgical rituals, attached to the veneration of the Sacred Heart, Our Lady of Lourdes, the Miraculous Medal, and such popular new saints as Joan of Arc (canonized in 1920) and Thérèse of Lisieux (the Little Flower of Jesus, canonized in 1925). Among Catholics, signs of these cults became ubiquitous features not only of church ritual but of work and home environments: "With each new devotion," McDannell writes, "the symbols of that devotion were made into statuary, medals, pendants, and pictures. If Catholics could not manage to get their special saint or Virgin into the church, they could place visual reminders of their devotions in church meeting rooms, hallways, hospitals, or homes" (170). A lively market in saints' images flourished: a Barclay Street advertisement from 1908 eagerly offers "special statues of any Saint sculptured on short notice" (quoted on 169). Even small Catholic congregations labored to make their altars splendid with polychrome statues, candles, flowers, linen, and lace, to give themselves a foretaste of their communities' vision of heavenly glories, and many church members erected little altars and shrines at home or at school.

Henry Darger was in many ways an entirely typical participant in this densely materialized devotional culture. He collages holy-card images of the Sacred Heart and various manifestations of the Virgin Mary into some of his drawings, and he organizes some of his narratives around special rituals such as the veneration of the Blessed Sacrament in Benediction or the Forty Hours devotion. Photographs taken of his room soon after he vacated it show a small mantelpiece crowded with home-size statues of Jesus, Our Lady of Lourdes, and a chromolithograph of the Infant Jesus of Prague, alongside various items of nondevotional bric-a-brac and photos. Similarly, next to his worktable, the upper half of a door is covered with illustrated religious calendars, Catholic magazine covers, and images of Jesus and the reigning pope, alongside pictures of children and dogs. One notes the same kinds of juxtapositions among his small collection of books, which included some of the most popular children's books and some of the reigning classic depictions of modern childhood and orphanhood available in English: the Wizard of Oz and its sequels, Heidi and its sequels, The Old Curiosity Shop and Great Expectations—but also The Pious Guide, St. Basil's Hymnal, The School of Jesus Crucified, and Blind Agnese; or, The Little Spouse of the Blessed Sacrament. One of the rare features of Darger's work is the extensive use by a highly intelligent, disciplined, and artistically gifted person of such popular religious narratives and images to explore what may have often seemed to him to be potentially overwhelmingly strong feelings, desires, or memories.

I began this chapter by recalling my own immersion as a small child in the rather demonic heroics of virgin martyrdom in order to remind myself as well as my readers not only that Darger's world of martyrs may not be as remote from our own era as we may tend to think it is, but also to remind ourselves that his apparent fascination with femininity and scenes of extreme cruelty and violence, far from having been (or having been only) some personal eccentricity of his, was the result of his having very much been a product of the devotional and spiritual tendencies of the Roman Catholic Church of the first half of the twentieth century. In repeatedly adverting to figures of youthful femininity, exposed and curiously gendered bodies, and scenes of intense cruelty visited on the very young, Darger may be understood to have been a participant in an extremely long-established set of cultural practices—ones that for well over a millennium constituted one of the most prestigious and highly respected modes of literary and visual representation. This was the narrative of martyrdom of female virgins, which preoccupied and inspired a number of long arcs of cultural production, ranging from the Acts of the virgin martyrs of the third and fourth centuries (circulated by the cults of Saints Felicity, Perpetua, Agnes, Catherine of Alexandria, and Thecla, among many others) to many of the mystery plays of the Middle Ages and Chaucer's "Second Nun's Tale," and well beyond.

It may surprise even many students of English literature to learn that, far from disappearing from the English theater at the time of the Reformation, virgin-martyr dramas continued to be written by influential playwrights and poets into the modern era, including Thomas Dekker's *The Virgin Martyr* of the early 1620s, which is about Saint Dorothy, and John Dryden's *Tyrannick Love; or, The Royal Martyr* of 1670, which is about Saint Catherine of Alexandria. And far from disappearing from English literature in the later modern period, the virgin-martyr narrative was once again taken up by some of the key architects of early mass culture for Christian readers—most notably in Cardinal Wiseman's *Fabiola* (1855) and John Henry Newman's *Callista* (1858), both of which were designed by their respective prelate authors as models of the use of popular historical fiction (which had been pioneered by Sir Walter Scott and his contemporaries a generation before) for new modes of mass religious pedagogy. Well-worn copies of both of these Victorian virgin-martyr romance novels still survived in the modest lending libraries of the small Catholic churches that my extended family attended in northeastern Oklahoma into the 1960s. Darger the omnivorous reader might have easily come across copies of these and similar books in the libraries of the Catholic hospitals where he worked and the neighborhood church he attended. The magazines and pamphlets he picked up there participated actively and enthusiastically in maintaining and transmitting the veneration of the virgin martyrs, from those of the Roman persecutions of the early church to such highly publicized cults as that of the twentieth-century Saint Maria Goretti (a "martyr for chastity" at age twelve in 1902, canonized in 1950), who had been born only a year or two before Darger was.

Although the violence with which Darger depicts Glandelinian soldiers martyring many of his heroines will probably remain unequivocally appalling to almost all his readers, becoming aware of the persistence of gory details of extreme cruelty and violence as an apparently indispensable feature of martyr narrative in general and of virgin-martyr narrative in particular may make some difference in the nature and quality of one's response to it. In her 1999 study of the popular medieval "theater of cruelty" of the martyrs and their legends, the cultural historian Jody Enders surveys and critiques the extensive scholarship on the "special effects" that were used in staging the frequent scenes of the tortures of martyrs, of the bodies of saints being beaten, broken, stabbed, burned, dismembered, and roasted alive, in performances of the execution of Saint Lawrence, or "deprived of [their] breasts," in the martyrdoms of Saints Agatha and Barbara.[3] In performing such central scenes from the life of Christ as Herod's Massacre of the Innocents, practitioners of medieval and early Renaissance stagecraft employed "fake blood, soft clubs, dummies, dolls, and mannequins . . . [in order] to render violence, torture, and death as realistically as possible."[4] Darger's substitution of his Glandelinian hordes for the stock tyrant Herod, European theater's ubiquitous villain from the medieval to the baroque stage, in his own recurrent revisions of the massacre is perhaps the most obvious point of contact between his "martyr theater" and earlier ones, which similarly depended on devotional narrative and liturgical ritual for much of their matter and manner. Even the disemboweling on which Darger's scenes of martyrdom often focus—something that may strike most readers as all but unrepresentable onstage—had been fully anticipated by earlier martyr plays; other historians of the medieval and early-modern theater refer to such scenes as having been enacted in martyr plays about Saints Barnabas and Denis.[5]

Even the specter of eroticized violence that haunts Darger's work has been a recognized feature of virgin-martyr narrative since its inception in the classical world. Until recently it was standard practice for students of the matter to recognize—if only to deplore—some degree of prurience in some modern readers' responses to the combination of such common features of virgin-martyr narrative as female nudity and scenes of extreme violence and cruelty. But scholars of late antiquity have in recent years become more forthright about acknowledging the unstable mixture of registers of piety and pathos, on the one hand, and, on the other, the varying degrees of erotic provocation, first to spectators and then to readers, that characterize even the earliest accounts of virgin martyrdom from the third and fourth centuries, each as the acts of Saints Felicitas, Perpetua, Paul, and Thecla.[6] Rather than representing some kind of inherently nonerotic text that has been corrupted or degraded by sexualization at the hands of some modern readers, virgin-martyr narratives have long commonly featured an unstabilizable erotic component.

Darger's Girl Martyrs: Jennie Anges and Annie Aronburg

We have already briefly considered the story of the boy martyr Tarsicius, who sacrifices his life in order to protect the consecrated communion hosts he is carrying from the pagan mob.

Darger retells the story of Tarsicius in a way that fuses some of the main elements of its plot with motifs from a lot of the girl virgin-martyr stories, of which Saint Agnes's is the best known. He does so at considerable length and in predictably gory detail, in book 9 of *In the Realms of the Unreal*, where it becomes the story of a six-year-old girl named Jennie Anges ("Agnes" with two letters inverted, or "Angels" with a letter omitted), whose body is literally pulled apart by cruel Glandelinian soldiers who would wrest from her the ciborium she carries and the consecrated communion wafers it contains, and desecrate them. The tale of little Jennie Anges provides a characteristic example of Darger's version of martyr narrative in *In the Realms of the Unreal*. Finding herself in a locale under attack by evil Glandelinian forces, six-year-old Jennie Anges's ultrapious thoughts are "not for her own safty [sic] but for the safty [sic] of the Dear God she loved." She rushes to the local church and takes the vessel containing consecrated communion hosts from the tabernacle, with the intention of protecting them from the "profaning and insulting" behavior they are likely to receive from the invaders. These soldiers, the narrator tells us, are likely to treat the hosts "in a way that would be a mortal sin to relate in writing or explaining in words, an example worse than acts of immodesty to the Holy Eucharist." Overtaken by the soldiers while still in church, Jennie Anges attempts to conceal the sacred vessel by folding her arms across her breast, momentarily creating a striking tableau: "So delicately formed she looked like some celestial angels standing before the altar. In fact," the narrator adds, "she was already marked for heaven."[7]

Several curious features of this opening scene of the story deserve remark. The child's first thoughts are said to be prompted by her concern not for her own "saf[e]ty" but for that of God himself. Although the narrator goes on to say that Jennie Anges is determined to protect the consecrated hosts from desecration, the actual desire motivating the child appears to be grounded in a sense that God and the sacred objects through which he manifests himself to people are so vulnerable to profanation and insult that he must depend on the death-defying heroics of little girls to protect and rescue them. The narrator, seemingly like the small child, cannot articulate what the alleged threat to God in the consecrated hosts is supposed to be, except by periphrasis and by repeating the words of others—hence the circumlocutions of "she had heard from eye witnesses that the Glandelinians would commit the first act of profaning and insulting the Sacred Heart Host in a way that would be a mortal sin to relate in writing or explaining in words, an example worse than acts of immodesty to the Holy Eucharist." Although as she adopts a protective posture toward the hosts as the soldiers approach her, she looks as "delicately formed" as "some celestial angels," and the narrator announces that "she was already marked for heaven." In other words, she is "already marked" for immediate martyrdom. Part of that marking resides in her very name, which evokes not only "angels" but also "Agnes," most celebrated of early Christian girl martyrs, whose name in turn yields *agnus*, Latin for (sacrificial) lamb.

The Glandelinians leap on Jennie Anges "with wild yells," "determined to rob her of her treasure":

> The wretches tugged violently and furiously at her arms, they pulled with all their might, they tore her clothes till she was completely naked, they showered blows upon her, cursed her, strangled her, pulled out her tongue, hair, and eyelashes, and kicked her in the stomach, and struck her in the face and jaw with their fist, and pulled out her hair, and tortured her most horribly, but those delicate arms did not move. They kicked her in the most delicate parts of her body, hit her in the side of her belly with

straps, and scourged her right before the altar but in vain. A strength and bravery from on high was given to the delicate child, and during all the excruciating torture, and bleeding from innumerable wounds, and in the desperate struggle she did not yield.

The first two sentences here both take the rhetorical form of, "The soldiers did everything they could imagine to injure and overcome the child, but they were nevertheless unable to accomplish their main objective, to prise the sacred vessel from the child's arms." The third sentence explains why: Jennie Anges has been imbued with a divine "strength and bravery" exceeding even the furious physical power of the band of soldiers.

In the ensuing paragraph, the violators intensify their attack on every surface of the child martyr's body, turning it into an attack on the integrity of the body itself, an intensification that is marked by a passage from the outside to the inside of the body: "At last an infuriated ruffian fell[ed] her with a blow of the heavy musket butt, and the others completed the work with their bayonets, literally laying her body open. They even tried to rip apart her chest and did so in their efforts to tear it loose, even tore out her heart and entrails and tried to cut the arms asunder. . . . [Darger's ellipses]. In death as in life however the faithful child kept her desperate grasp upon the ciborium, nor could all the united efforts of the wild Glandelinians tear it away." God performs a miracle through the Glandelinian soldiers' dismemberment of Jennie Anges's body: it is (as the narrator insists) "literally" ripped open and its contents dispersed, but no amount of human force can pry apart the little arms protecting the ciborium. The furious soldiers throw the corpse into the nearby river, the sacred vessel still "safe" in the otherwise completely ravaged body. Some time later, the Vivian Girls—who make several successful rescues in In the Realms of "the Blessed Sacrament" without suffering the martyr's death that comes to Jennie Anges—come across her grave, which is surmounted by a "large tombstone" that reads: "Here sleeps in the Lord / Little Jennie Anges, aged six. / THE LITTLE GIRL MARTYR / who died in the most terrible tortures / in defense of the / MOST BLESSED SACRAMENT." "As they stood by the grave," the narrator continues, "never had poor Violet and her sisters looked so beautiful. They kneel and kiss the grave, weeping and murmuring 'Anges' over and over."

The nature of the aestheticized payoff at the end of this narrative is clear. Although Jennie Anges has ostensibly perished in terrible violence in order to "protect" her beloved Lord's "safety," the reader may suspect that she has actually done so in order "literally" to ground yet another sublime photo-op for the Vivians, who had never looked so good as they did standing at her grave. The only partially sublimated sexual violence of the attack on Jenny Anges ("The Poor child however was surprised before she had time to conceal her treasure," "They were determined to rob her of her treasure," "they tore her clothes till she was completely naked," "They kicked her in the most delicate part of her legs and body") is all but completely buried and encrypted in the remarkably beautiful appearance that is attributed to the Vivian Girls at this point. But their weeping, kneeling, stooping over, and kissing the grave (the "ground") bears some partial witness to the hyperviolent erotics of the martyrdom of Jennie Anges. Erich Auerbach explicates the etymology of "martyr" not only in relation to the Greek for "witness," the commonplace derivation of the word, but specifically to the act of witnessing "something like pure suffering."[8] But (to paraphrase Mae West), "purity," as we have seen, has little or nothing to do with the suffering that we witness in the story of Jennie Anges. The obscene or scandalous feature of the narrative is perhaps not so much the strong hints of violent erotics that hover over it, nor even what is supposed to be the aesthetic payoff at its end, but the "an-esthetic" miracle of the little girl's superstoic ability to keep her arms folded over the sacred vessel not only while her body is torn apart and open, but even afterward, in death. Jennie Anges's miraculous arms are those not of an angel but of a statue of an angel, and her body one in which rigor mortis begins to set in *before* death. The miracle that surrounds her death is that part or all of her was dead from the time (or even before it?) when she assumed her "delicate" and "angelic" posture before the altar—as the ominous phrase has it, "already marked for heaven." Long before the reader realizes it, her little body has miraculously become the "large tombstone" that memorializes her in a way that compels the Vivian sisters to stand over it, as the narrator says, "with their souls in their eyes." Perhaps Jennie Anges has to die such a horrific death because her story is preinscribed in the legends of the martyrs, the canonical site of such stories of the violation by torture of the pious. As a scriptive form, legend is always already engraved in stone.

I have begun with the story of Jennie Anges because it is not only a representative one but a narratively compact one. The other Dargerian revision of the standard girl-martyr legend I want to consider is that of Annie Aronburg, which is much less clearly or efficiently narrated. Rather, it occupies a diffuse and oblique relation to narration. Indeed, it is presented as constituting the engine driving the entire massive narrative, for it is what Darger himself christened "the Aronburg mystery" that is allegedly at the heart of the labyrinthine story of In the Realms. This is the "mystery" supposedly surrounding the identities of Annie Aronburg's killers and, more specifically, surrounding the role of Darger's loss of a photograph of the dead girl in the escalation and prolongation of the Glandeco-Angelinian war. Just as Jennie Anges is "already marked for heaven" at the beginning of her story, Annie Aronburg has always already been martyred in In the Realms. Somewhat conflicting accounts of her death and of the identities of her killers circulate through the story, as do her memory, her ghost, and a number of surviving relatives of hers, several of whom play major roles in the grand narrative (her sister, Angeline Aronburg, succeeds her as one of the top leaders of the girl scouts and becomes in the course of the narrative almost an "eighth Vivian sister," and her uncle General Concentinian Aronburg eventually rises to a position of command over all the Christian armies). But it is above all Darger's loss of his photograph of her that is said to impel much of the narrative of the war and to constitute by itself the portentous-sounding "Aronburg mystery." "Mystery" is a particularly resonant term in the context of Darger's revisionary version of girl-martyr theater, comprehending as it does the medieval sense of the term encapsulated in the phrase "mystery play"—allegorical dramas often based on the sufferings of Christ from the Massacre of the Innocents to the crucifixion, or the sufferings of martyred saints—and the modern term "mystery," which denotes one of the most pervasive genres of popular fiction. Mysteries had become such a popular form in the years in which Darger started writing In the Realms that even such early-childhood book series as The Bobbsey Twins, of which Darger possessed at least a couple of volumes, began to feature detective plots.

At the age of eight or nine, Annie Aronburg is already recognized as one of the most successful child leaders of the rebellion, and she is assassinated by one or more of the Glandelinians because of both her military and political importance and her extraordinary piety.[9] What Darger calls "the Aronburg mystery" is, as both MacGregor and Michael Bonesteel have demonstrated, actually a kind of two-phase mystification, the first part of which is a conventional whodunit ("Who killed Annie Aronburg?") and the second part of which is a set of questions about the nature of the connection between her murder and the turning of the war against her side, and, more specifically (and obsessively), between Darger's loss of a photograph (or two) of her and the drastic downturn in the fortunes of the Christian side in the war that ensues. MacGregor discusses Darger's own apparent awareness of the frustration and hostility that others may feel about the alleged link he persists in asserting in the narrative between his loss of the photograph and the increasing likelihood of the Christian forces' loss of the war. At one point, two Abbieannian generals discuss Darger's "claim that the loss [of the photograph] is responsible for the calamity" their armies have been experiencing. "The man must be a nut," one of them opines, "for how could the loss of a picture be responsible for the disaster? Pictures don't cause terrible battles like this." "His statements show him to be a maniac of the queerest kind," the man concludes. "It may be a positive fact that he lost the pictures, but it is all nonsense about their causing the disaster" (497). Near the end of the massive narrative, the Vivian Girls and their protectors are still quite confused about the nature of the "mystery": "But what in the name of heaven is the situation really about?" Catherine asks. "What is the mystery of the Aronburg situation anyway?" Their guardian, young Captain Jack Evans, responds, "No one can solve the mystery and probably never will. It's about as hard to solve as the Divinity it seems" (501). In another scene set late in the war, another of the Christian generals ponders the terrible possibility that their side may lose: "'This is all on account of that Darger and his old picture,' he said bitterly. 'I wonder how it could be recovered?'" (503).

Although the photograph never is recovered, Annie Aronburg's body is. Like the sanctified bodies of saints in general, Annie Aronburg's is said to remain "undecayed" long after her death. The Christian boy scout Walter Starring explains to the Vivian Girls that it is "by the power of God" and "for the purpose of its being discovered" that the body has been preserved from decay. With Starring as their guide, the children find the body "lying naked and outstretched on the gravel just as it had been left. To their surprise the intestines were gone, only the flesh and bones being left. The worms had only eaten the inside organs and left the rest so that everything was empty inside" (508). In another episode (in volume 11 of In the Realms), a soldier presents the children with a set of parcels containing various internal organs that had been taken from Annie Aronburg's body and a "prescription" on a large yellow sheet of paper enjoining the recipients of these "terrible relics" not to replace them in the interior of the corpse but to "retain them" until Annie's killer or killers are "brought to justice" (the command is said to have been written by a Blengin, one of the benevolent winged creatures who are charged with protecting the children, at least some of the time). Rather than being told to reunite corpse and internal organs for decent burial, as one might expect, the children are strictly commanded to keep the "terrible relics" separate from the corpse as long as Annie Aronburg's killers remain at large.

Again manifesting saintly qualities, Annie Aronburg visits Darger three times after her death in the form of a spiritual apparition. Several times, she reproaches him for the way he has turned the war against the Christian forces out of rage over the loss of his photograph of her, and she entreats him to desist. "You alone have the situation of both sides in your power," she tells him. Drawn as he is to her, Darger finds himself unable to yield (512, 516). At the end of In the Realms, General Hanson (the character who had once opined that Darger "must be a nut" to believe that there was a causal connection between his loss of a photograph and the Christian armies' bad fortune) comes riding up to "general Henry Darger" to inquire: "Do you fully know any more of this Aronburg mystery, H? How about the return of the lost photograph? Did you not find it yet?" "No sir," he replies, "and I'm sure that I'll never find it. I've found all my stolen property but that. The picture amounts to nothing, and neither its loss. All that is necessary is the destruction of the remainder of her [Annie Aronburg's] murderers" (519). Here, Darger through one of his alter egos expresses himself willing to "get over" his rage at God for not answering his prayers for the return of the lost photograph, and to (as it were) rejoin the more conventional revenge or return-to-justice plot that drives the other "good" characters in In the Realms. Before accepting his conciliatory gesture at face value, I want to think a bit more about what is at stake in "the Aronburg mystery."

Let us look a little more closely at the martyr legends Darger is rewriting in his respective treatments of Jennie Anges and Annie Aronburg. Although, as I have mentioned, Jennie Anges shows traces in her second name of "angel[s]" and the early Christian martyr Agnes and, through her, the agnus or sacrificial lamb, we should also note that through her first name she is also associated with two other characters in In the Realms, Jennie Sanders, a little girl who is driven mad by suffering (564), and Jennie Turmer, a girl who "bobs" her hair and cross-dresses as a boy in her attempt to escape to the Christian army (526). In the same way that "Anges" evokes "Agnes," "Jennie" evokes "Joan," and Jennie Turmer's cutting her hair and adopting male dress in wartime alludes directly to the legend of Joan of Arc, the most celebrated of female martyrs in the early twentieth century and one who was especially widely invoked in both American and French pious (and patriotic) writing during the First World War, the decade when Darger began writing and produced much of the verbal text of In the Realms. As a maid, or maiden, and a virgin who assumed men's clothing and led a medieval Christian nation to military victory, only to be condemned and burned at the stake by her enemies at the age of nineteen, Joan the triumphant and martyred girl commander is an obvious model for the military and Christian religious heroics of Darger's heroines. Popular devotion to Joan, already at a height in the First World War, when she was invoked as an emblem of victory for war-torn France, culminated in her canonization in 1920, five hundred years after her death. The international Catholic cult of Joan of Arc, then, was peaking during the first two decades that Darger worked on In the Realms, and during the time that he appears to have completed the bulk of the writing. The process of assimilating the image of the saint into American popular culture was proceeding apace at the same time, as "Joan of Arc" appeared as a brand name for various products and as the heroine of one of the first big-budget Cecil B. DeMille film extravaganzas, Joan the Woman (1917).

But in considering the girl heroines of Darger's saga, one notices that it is Annie (and her surviving sister, Angeline) rather than Jennie who are most Joan-like. At the same time that one notices that Jennie Anges's initials are the same as Joan of Arc's, one may also notice the assonance of Annie (and Angie, as well as the name of their other sister, Anna) with Jennie as well as with Joan. Nor should one overlook the similarly close assonance of the name Henry with both Annie and Jennie. The similarity of these names to each other and the way all of them proliferate across a significant portion of the major characters of In the Realms betoken a close identification on "Henry's" part—at least at the level of the name—with the various Annies and Jennies who undergo martyrdom in his text, as well as with the virgin martyrs Agnes and Joan, whose names Darger's heroines cite and revise.

When another of Darger's Jennies—this one Jennie Turmer—first cross-dresses, she expresses concern to Angelinia Aronburg about whether she will be able to impersonate a boy convincingly. The knowing Angelinia casually tells her not to "exert" herself overmuch trying to impersonate a butch boy: "There is now and then sissy young boys who act like girls you know, and I think therefore it would be better and easier [for you] to act like a boy who is in the class of sissies" (526). MacGregor speculates about whether Darger himself had been included "in the class of sissies" by his peers (535), and—given his bookishness, combined with the weird hand gestures and vocalizations in which he is said to have engaged as a child—it is hard to see how Darger would not have been taken by at least some people to have been a particularly spooky kind of sissy. Part of the significance of the spectacularization of girlish bravado in In the Realms may be reparative in a somewhat displaced way: if little girls can not only show valor on the battlefield but can also, at least sometimes, outwit and even outmaneuver gangs of male bullies, maybe sissy boys have a chance in the battle of life, too—even though that chance does not appear to be explicitly enacted in the narrative. In Darger's retelling of the most popular boy martyr's story, the boy becomes a little girl.

After seeming to disappear into a largely forgotten past in the wake of the reforms of the Second Vatican Council, virgin-martyr narratives and images have reemerged in recent years (in both print and on the Internet) as one of the "retro" tendencies of some strands of Roman Catholic home schooling, in which a marked nostalgia for the more gothic extremes of cults of pious suffering (with Mel Gibson's film The Passion of the Christ representing an upper limit) stands as part of a more generalized nostalgia for the antimodernist (and later also anticommunist) "church militant" that dominated Roman Catholicism for much of the past two centuries. But Darger's interest in such ghastly seeming phenomena as child sacrifice, child torture, and other kinds of extreme violence and abuse bespeaks not only an investment in the ancient and even archaic past of the Roman Catholic virgin-martyr legend. Some of what many viewers may prefer to see as particularly bizarre and idiosyncratic aspects of Darger's personal fixations no longer seem inexplicable or out of place in our contemporary world, in which child soldiers, the theft of human organs, torture, and current practices of martyrdom and self-martyrdom (such as suicide bombings) have lamentably become fixtures of the global political scene. To a disturbing degree today, practices of martyrdom and extreme (and lethal) forms of self-sacrifice have—a generation after Darger's death in 1973—refused to stay in the "retro" box where we might like to consign them and have resumed their place in the forefront of contemporary life. The medical anthropologist Nancy Scheper-Hughes and her colleagues have drawn worldwide attention to the black market in illegally harvested human organs, and the feminist scholar Claudia Castañeda has explored what she sees as the complex truth at work in the widely circulated and reported rumors of organ theft from the bodies of children in contemporary Guatemala and other places.[10] Aspects of Darger's work that may look like a throwback to much earlier, even archaic times and places—his fascination with the extraction of organs from the bodies of young people, especially girls, and their bloody sacrifice—has in another way come in recent years to take on a ghastly new kind of recognizability. This uncanny and unwelcome kind of familiarity in our own era of torture, child soldiers, and young political martyrs makes the artist in some ways our contemporary.[11]

Trauerspiel: *Darger and Mourning-Play*

Early in the introduction to this book, I discussed the sometimes serious nature of play, especially children's play, and suggested that the reader and viewer of Darger's work can often see him engaging in forms of highly serious play with the apparently incongruous combinations of material that he brings together. In concluding this chapter, I want to take this notion a step further and consider how play and not only seriousness but downright sorrow endlessly come together, separate, and recombine in the writing and drawing of In the Realms. The *faux*-upbeat tone of classic children's series narration—especially of those many children's books, including some of Darger's favorites (such as those by G. A. Henty) that present the "adventures" of boy combatants in war—is quite compatible with the alternating and sometimes simultaneous tones of doughty earnestness ("now be a good little soldier") and pious lamentation ("They [the Vivian Girls] kneel and kiss the grave, weeping and murmuring [Jennie Anges's name] over and over") that characterize Darger's work. Early in the twentieth century, during some of the same years that Darger was writing In the Realms, Walter Benjamin produced a failed dissertation that has eventually become one of the most influential critical studies of the twentieth century. This is his Origin of German Tragic Drama, his study of the (even to many Germanists) obscure form of the baroque Trauerspiel (mourning-play). In this study, Benjamin argues that these plays, written by such authors as Andreas Gryphius (1616–64) and filled with bombastic speeches and bloody and often grotesque conflicts between tyrants and martyrs, require a different mode of understanding from classical tragedy and the literature derived from it. If (at least since Aristotle) Oedipus has been the quintessential tragic hero, Herod the Massacrer of the Innocents has been the quintessential blustering tyrant who presides over his own and his many victims' ruin in the mourning-play. According to Benjamin, high tragedy is about its mythological protagonists' transcending their fates, while mourning-play is about all-too-real historical figures, trapped in epochs of failed sovereignty or endless, disastrous, hyperviolent war, experiencing the terrible immanence of their existence and succumbing to the ruination that is their destiny.[12]

But they do not do so without complaint. The forms the complaint takes are not the resounding, eloquent, uplifting accents of classical tragedy as it reaches its dramatic and ethical climaxes; they are noisy, fitful, confused, tearful, choking, repetitive, ridiculous, bombastic outbursts of sound, alternately furious and terrified. In other words, they are the very tones of Darger's (often bathetically) sorrowful martyr theater. Gryphius, the stereotypical author of the *trauerspiel*, was orphaned as a child and driven from his homeland early in the catastrophic and violent Thirty Years' War (1618–48)—an initiation into life that no doubt would have interested Darger.[13] The angry and chaotic realms that the victim characters of the *Trauerspiel* traverse resonate with some of the most familiar (and disturbing) features of Darger's "realms of the unreal." Writing during the early years of the short-lived Weimar Republic, Benjamin in the *Origin* looked back and recognized the unstable but fascinating contours of an aesthetic formation grounded in desperate and raging sorrow from the German past, one with a terribly and uncannily proleptic grasp of kinds of mass horrors that lay in wait for millions of Jews and other Europeans of the time. In writing the *Origin*, Benjamin eventually brought back to international critical attention a long-forgotten literature of the ridiculous and atrocious politics and culture of all-out war and systemic social violence. His is one of the few literary-critical programs that seems potentially able to help us understand and account for some of the exorbitant energies of Darger's narrative and pictorial accounts of the victims and perpetrators of genocide and total war.[14] To help illuminate some of the particularly harrowing ironies of the place of children in "sorrow play," I turn in the next chapter to considering the potential relation of Darger's *In the Realms* to the most celebrated chronicles of war by child authors in the canon of modern juvenilia.

Chapter 2

ROTTEN TRUTHS, WASTED

LIVES, SPOILED COLLECTIONS

DARGER'S WORK AND THE

BRONTËS' JUVENILIA

> Fantasied universes of self-contained mean-
> ing are the very finest and noblest substi-
> tutes we can ever devise for that precise and
> loving insight into the nooks and crannies of
> the real that must be forever denied us.
> —Edward Sapir, "Psychiatric and Cultural
> Pitfalls in the Business of Getting a Living"

Adult Juvenilia

Henry Darger's *In the Realms of the Unreal*, with its odd and otherworldly combination of fairy tale and children's adventure story with sometimes grim
and virtually endless chronicles of suffering, separation, and loss in war, and
of intense, protracted, and unfulfilled desires, has reminded some readers
of the Ramayana and the Mahabharata (relocated to Oz). A number of other
commentators have noted some resemblances between Darger's project and
the celebrated juvenilia of the Brontë siblings, Charlotte, Branwell, Emily,
and Anne.[1] The analogy has been made mostly in passing; I want to pursue it
in some detail in this chapter. First I will consider some of the ways in which
the Brontës' immense output of so-called juvenilia from childhood well into
adulthood appears to have constituted for them a vast and in some ways end-

less project of mourning and lamenting the deaths of their mother and elder sisters. I want to look in greater detail at some (I think) especially telling resemblances between Darger's and Branwell Brontë's respective projects. Although all four Brontë siblings continued to produce juvenilia well into early adulthood, Branwell remained involved in the chronicles of war and palace intrigue that he and his sister Charlotte had created together as children and adolescents well after she had turned away from what they called "the infernal world" of Angria and set her sights on establishing herself as a professional author and full participant in the public sphere of the novel.

Between Darger's and Branwell Brontë's respective "infernal worlds" (or "realms of the unreal") there turn out to be extensive and peculiar connections. Although Darger used as many of his most vital resources what were then new forms of mass culture, such as cheap religious pamphlets and printed images, children's book series, and newspaper comic strips, his work also drew deeply and extensively on some of the same kinds of cultural resources—middle- and highbrow—on which Charlotte and Branwell Brontë had drawn in creating the imaginary kingdoms of Glasstown and Angria. Chief among these resources was the new style of military and colonialist journalism that the two elder Brontë children greedily absorbed from the pages of their father's copies of Blackwood's Magazine, which featured detailed and often grisly accounts of British colonial wars in Africa, failed polar expeditions, and the Peninsular Wars (also depicted in some of Goya's most disturbing images, which have been compared to Darger's).[2] The next generation of "war correspondents" produced the stirring accounts of US Civil War battles that Darger read so absorptively as a child. And the generation after that wrote the narratives of battlefield slaughter, displacement of entire civilian populations, and sufferings and heroism of masses of war orphans in the First World War that served Darger as primary source material during the early years of composing In the Realms.

In considering Darger's paintings and narratives of war "in the realms of the unreal" as a fluid series of virtually endless "mourning-plays," I emphasized in the previous chapter their relation to martyr theater. By juxtaposing some of the same features of Darger's work—its extreme and grotesque violence, and its haunting and mournful tone—with some of the same characteristics in Branwell Brontë's art and writing, I hope to make clearer the character of In the Realms as a soldier's tale, albeit an immensely strange one that finds its inspiration in the military heroism of little girls and espouses a vision of glory in combat that is shrouded at all points with an overwhelming sense of the exorbitant cruelty of warfare and the piteousness of victimhood. The first tale I turn to here is a famous one about a set of toy soldiers.

The Revivifying Powers of Endless Tales of Infernal Grief

As the story goes, the gift of a set of toy soldiers from their father Patrick Brontë to Branwell in 1826 had initially stimulated the children (Charlotte was then ten, Branwell nine, Emily eight, and Anne six) to begin making "plays" about their new playthings, whom they called "the young men." Within a few years, the "plays," which appear to have been primarily oral and enactive in form, had developed into an ever-increasing number of miniature magazines and books, the imagining and writing of which soon became and long remained a consuming project for all four children, individually and collectively. Charlotte christened her favorite soldier the Duke of Wellington and Branwell named his Bonaparte, after the two superhuman heroes of the late wars; after some initial casting about, Emily and Anne named theirs Ross and Parry, respectively, after the pioneering Arctic explorers of the time. In the children's play, these military leaders and their forces began to colonize parts of West Africa and to build a magnificent colonial capitol there, Glasstown, which the Brontës' biographer, Juliet Barker, has called "a heady mixture of London, Paris and Babylon."[3] Wearying of what they saw as their brother's obsession with parliamentary politics and, worse, the extreme violence of combat, Emily and Anne soon seceded from the Glasstown project and launched Gondal, their own imaginary kingdom, and its chronicles (unfortunately, only a small part of the Gondal material—mostly some of the verse sections—is extant; only a few very brief summary segments of prose have survived). Transforming the kingdom of Glasstown into the colonial empire of Angria, Charlotte and Branwell continued to collaborate with each other for many years. At least in the early years, as far as bloodshed and "coarseness" were concerned, she seemed more than willing to follow his lead; "the gory fights between the Marquis [of Douro, elder son of the Duke of Wellington] and his enemies in [Charlotte's] *Something about Arthur*, for example, rival even the most violent scenes in Branwell's *Letters from an Englishman*," writes Christine Alexander, the chief editor of Charlotte's juvenilia.[4] Although she did not remain as attracted to scenes of mayhem in battle or parliamentary debate as Branwell was, Charlotte does appear to have shared some of his fascinations, such as that with intense fraternal envy and competitiveness, and she continued after the early period to produce in association with him thousands of pages chronicling the machinations of their primary alter egos in the juvenilia, the rivalrous pair composed of Wellington's son Arthur Wellesley (Charlotte's), who becomes the fabulously glamorous Duke of Zamorna and King of Angria, and Alexander Percy or "Rogue" (Branwell's), who becomes the no less glamorous and tormented Earl of Northangerland, a figure who repeatedly embroils the kingdom in bloody civil war. Sir Walter Scott's highland romances of star-crossed lovers seem to have set the primary tone for life in Emily and Anne's Gondal; Byron's poems about Luciferian men and their tortured public and private careers (as well as the personal example of such an existence that Byron embodied for his contemporaries) dominate the history of Charlotte and Branwell's Angria.

The Brontë siblings may have set the limit for how old an author may be while still producing so-called juvenilia, for chronologically coming of age did little or nothing to staunch the great flow of narrative they had begun to produce in childhood. Nearly two decades after inaugurating their "plays," as they passed into their late twenties, they continued to find compelling Angria and Gondal—"the infernal world" or "the world below," as they sometimes called it. In 1845, for example, Emily and Anne—then twenty-seven and twenty-five, respectively, and on the threshold of commencing their careers as professional novelists—passed the two days of a train journey role-playing together, pretending that they were a whole cast of royalist prisoners escaping from Gondal.[5] Branwell, too, continued to write juvenilia throughout his twenties. According to Alexander, even Charlotte, the first of the siblings to attempt to put Angria behind her, appears to have continued writing about the imaginary kingdom until she was twenty-four. The famous manuscript that critics have called her "farewell to Angria" ends with this sentence: "Still, I long to quit for awhile that burning clime where we have sojourned too long—its skies flame—the glow of sunset is always upon it—the mind would cease from excitement and turn now to a cooler region where the dawn breaks grey and sober, and the coming day for a time at least is subdued by clouds."[6] Angria has become too hot and bright to be borne in Charlotte's migrainous vision of the imaginary African landscape that has at length become stuck in her mind's eye in the perpetual lurid orange glow of some endless tropical day (as hallucinated from the gray and mossy hills of Yorkshire).

During the years of her own late adolescence and early adulthood, as she continued writing linking and overlapping narratives with her brother, Charlotte eventually began to work out her own special fascinations with the stories she found to tell of a long series of women, low- as well as highborn, who seem mesmerized by the erotic appeal of one or the other of her and Branwell's Byronic duo. Brontë scholars have until quite recently tended to treat Charlotte's juvenilia as an adequate synechdoche for the "early" writings of all four siblings—an understandable response, given that little of her two sisters' early writing survives and that Branwell, unlike his three sisters, did not go on to become a celebrated author in his own right. Although a massive amount of his early writings are extant (comparable in quantity with Charlotte's), Branwell's juvenilia have only recently (1997–99) been edited and published in a scholarly edition.[7] The mainstream critics of Charlotte Brontë, from Winifred Gérin and Helene Moglen to Christine Alexander, have had essentially one story to tell about the relationship of her early writing to the novels she published, and it tends to be a highly teleological developmental narrative about her alleged repudiation of her "narcissistic," excessively romantic juvenilia in favor, ultimately, of the disciplined and sober ("mature") realism of *Jane Eyre* and *Villette*. Branwell has predictably been typecast as the "model failure" in this narrative, whose contrasting alleged inability to outgrow his penchant for writing lurid stories about his fantasies of fraternal treachery and grim and gruesome military struggles may have stunted his development as an artist and is of a piece with his (again, allegedly) addictive and pathological personality. Indeed, Branwell has in a sense become "the infernal world" that he and his sisters cultivated together, linked as his life has been with that phrase since the appearance of Daphne du Maurier's popular and influential study, *The Infernal World of Branwell Brontë*. As Charlotte's career is taken to represent with almost allegorical clarity the triumph of a woman writer's developing a practice of mature realism out of an infantile or adolescent addiction to romance, Branwell's has with similarly supposed clarity come to represent the tragedy of the man who is unable or unwilling to put away childish things and assume a properly realist aesthetic and a properly adult masculinity.

I want to turn at this point to consider an alternative body of scholarship on the Brontë siblings that tends to diminish, rather than to heighten and exaggerate, the gulf between their juvenilia and their "mature" writing, and between Branwell's writing and that of his sisters. Literary scholars and biographers who have focused more closely on the Brontës' early lives have in general tended to emphasize the continuities among the experiences of the four siblings as people who shared the loss of their mother and two older sisters while still small children—children who subsequently developed elaborate collaborative means for their attempts to come to terms (or refusal to come to terms) with these grievous early losses. The Brontës' mother died when Branwell was four, and the oldest sister Maria—who had for a while in some ways replaced the mother—died when he was not quite eight (coincidentally, Henry Darger sustained his most grievous losses at about the same ages, with the death of his mother just before he turned four, and his separation from his father when he was eight). The critic Kate Brown has written a compelling analysis of Charlotte Brontë's juvenilia, her "never-ending story" (the phrase occurs early in *Jane Eyre*), as an extended and elaborate practice of mourning in which the loss of the mother and of the second oldest sister, Elizabeth, both become concentrated in the children's mourning for Maria, their temporary substitute mother during their mother's final illness and after her death. Maria is also a key figure in this story, insofar as it was she who first led the children in the kind of "make-believe" enactments based on their shared reading that subsequently led to their "plays" about their toy soldiers and ultimately to the Glasstown, Gondal, and Angria chronicles.[8] I want especially to consider how Brown's analysis may need to be modified in some ways to account for the particular emphases in Branwell's juvenilia on grotesque violence and mass devastation, emphases it shares with some of Darger's work.

Brown's account of the juvenilia extends the way of thinking about it that was inaugurated by Fannie E. Ratchford in *The Brontës' Web of Childhood* (1941); Ratchford inaugurated a persistent substream of criticism that emphasizes the continuities between the juvenilia and the siblings' later work, rather than insisting on a dramatic rupture between them (and an invidious reading of the meaning of the alleged rupture). As Brown tells the story, the children carry out this project of mourning (which eventually grows into the sagas of Angria and Gondal) in relation to a very limited set of material objects: an old geography book that their father had once loaned to Maria—a fact that Maria had inscribed in the front of the book—and the aforementioned set of toy soldiers that their father had given Branwell and from which the children had each adopted a favorite. Charlotte tells the story in a memorandum she wrote in 1829, when she was twelve, titled "The History of the Year":

Once papa lent my sister Maria a book. It was an old geography, and she wrote on its blank leaf, "Papa lent me this book." The book is an hundred and twenty years old. It is at this moment lying before me while I write this. I am in the kitchen of the parsonage house, Haworth. Tabby the servant is washing up after breakfast, and Anne, my youngest sister (Maria was my eldest), is kneeling on a chair looking at some cakes which Tabby has been baking for us. Emily is in the parlour brushing it. Papa and Branwell are gone to Keighley. Aunt is upstairs in her room and I am sitting by the table writing this in the kitchen.[9]

One notable feature of this paragraph is the repetitive doubleness of its "homely" rhetoric: "Once papa lent my sister Maria a book" / "she wrote on its blank leaf, "Papa lent me this book"; "while I write this. I am in the kitchen" / "It [the old geography book] is at this moment lying before me while I write this" / "I am sitting by the table writing this in the kitchen." (Charlotte has perhaps already caught the trick of verbal echoing and doubling so effectively exploited throughout the King James Bible.) The doubling here is not simply verbal; it parallels the implicit doubling that occurs between the passage's charged figures of father and (now deceased) daughter and between deceased older sister and living younger sister. Maria's writing in the book in the past is somehow analogous with Charlotte's writing at the table in the present of the writing; the same book that was once received on loan from the father and inscribed with the fact by the now deceased older sister lies before the surviving sister as she writes in the present. I call the rhetoric "homely" not only because it is plain and domestic but also because, like much other "homely" rhetoric, it has a way of suddenly giving way to an *unheimlich* and uncanny rhetoric that, in this case, insists that the book lying before the writer on the table crucially and simultaneously both *is* and *is not* the same book that Maria Brontë once received and took as a mark of favor from and intellectual solidarity with their father. (I shall return in a moment to the question of how the book is and is not the same in the paragraph's doubling of it.)

After an intermediate paragraph recounting which newspapers and periodicals the family regularly read (two Tory papers and a Whig one, and *Blackwood's Magazine*, with its stable of provocative and pseudonymous writers whom the children especially admired and were already sedulously imitating, including "James Hogg, a man of most extraordinary genius, a Scottish shepherd"), Charlotte goes on to recount how "our plays were established." The first she calls the *Young Men's*; in giving a story of its origins, she tells what thereafter became the famous story of the gift of the toy soldiers who became "The Twelve," the heroes of the children's early sagas:

Papa brought Branwell some soldiers from Leed's. When Papa came home it was night and we were in bed, so next morning Branwell came to our door with a box of soldiers. Emily and I jumped out of bed and I snatched up one and exclaimed, "This is the Duke of Wellington! It shall be mine!" When I said this, Emily likewise took one and said it should be hers. When Anne came down she took one also. Mine was the prettiest of the whole and perfect in every part. Emily's was a grave-looking fellow. We called him "Gravey." Anne's was a queer little thing, very much like herself. He was called "Waiting Boy." Branwell chose "Bonaparte."[10]

Brown points out that the gift of the soldiers occurred about a year after Maria's death and may have actually been intended by their father and understood by the children as a way of marking the end of the family's first year of mourning—not necessarily to end mourning altogether, but to transpose it into a different key or mode. Brown argues—rightly, I think—that the old geography book and the set of toy soldiers circulate among the children as the material bases that ground a way not of ending but of perpetuating their grief for their sister. But this perpetuation of grief is one with a difference: this is a grief that can give renewed life of a kind both to the mourner and to the deceased. A kind of radical identification with a beloved object such as the old geography book—initially a sign of failed or blocked transmission between generations—becomes in practice a way for the mourner to gain, in the words of Emily Apter and William Pietz in *Fetishism as Cultural Discourse*, "an experience of his or her own living self through an impassioned response to the . . . object."[11] For Brown, the toy soldiers represent not the deadening effects of the inanimate corpse with which the mourners feel they must stop identifying lest they come to die too, but a form of "arrested life" (here, Brown borrows a phrase of Susan Stewart's). The "beloved object," the book or toy soldier (both given by their surviving parent), Brown writes, "translates grief not just into treasure but also into 'absurd satisfaction.'"[12] This "absurd satisfaction," as Brown presents it, is not so much a cure for grief as itself a form of grief that can be endlessly perpetuated, so compatible is it with both continuing mourning and a renewed sense of vitality.

In the first half of her discussion, Brown retains at least a nominal focus on the juvenilia as a collective enterprise, but as her analysis grows increasingly fine-grained in the second half, her focus shifts entirely to Charlotte. Brown ultimately analyzes only the psychic transformation experienced by the oldest surviving sister as the culmination of her mourning for her deceased oldest sister. What Brown does not note is that as Charlotte tells the story as early as 1829—only about four years after Maria's death—the allegedly failed transmission between "papa" and Maria that the book and its inscription mark has become what Charlotte represents as the entirely successful transmission of the role of the oldest sister from Maria to Charlotte, and the manifestation of its success is through the "new" oldest sister's placement at the heart of the family in the act of writing, while every other member performs some relatively uninteresting (albeit necessary) action or chore—from Tabby's washing up and Emily's brushing the parlor furniture to Patrick and Branwell's going into Keighley for the newspaper (other than Charlotte, only nine-year-old Anne, staring at the cakes, escapes chores). In the juvenile "History of the Year," Charlotte's vocation as a writer seems secured; her siblings' much less so—at least as the child Charlotte tells it. In trying to think about the distinct nature of Branwell's contribution to the siblings' juvenilia—as well as in trying to account for some striking resemblances between his work and Henry Darger's—we may need to revise somewhat Brown's schema of Charlotte Brontë's mourning, her learning to choose and to love (radically and in a sense irrationally) a small set of "beloved objects" that will enable her to value "arrested life" and to enjoy the "absurd satisfaction" that such a love can bring.

Another Toy Story: A Genius for Waste

In order to begin trying to effect this revision, let us turn to Branwell's retelling of the story of the gift of the toy soldiers. This occurs in "Introduction to the History of the Young Men," written over a year after Charlotte's version by Branwell, then thirteen:

> It was sometime in the summer of the year AD 1824 when I [then age seven] being desirous to possess a box of soldiers asked papa to buy me one which shortly afterwards he procured me from Bradford[.] They were 12 in number price 1s 6d and were the best I ever had[.] Soon after this I got from Keighly another set of the same number[.] These soldiers I kept for about a year untill [sic] either maimed lost burnt or destroyed by various casualties. . . . Now therefore not satisfied with what I had formerly got I purchased at Keighly a band of Turkish musicians which I continued to keep till the summer of AD 1825 when Charlotte and Emily returned from school where they had been during the days of my former sets[.]

I remained for 10 months after they had returned without any soldiers when on June the 5th AD 1826 papa procured me from Leeds another set (those were the 12s) which I kept for 2 years though 2 or 3 of them are in being at the time of my writing this (Dec 15 AD 1830)[.] Sometime in 1827 I bought another set of Turkish Musicians at Halifax and in 1828 I purchased the Last Box a band of Indians at Haworth[.] Both these I still keep. [H]ere now ends the catalogue of soldiers bought by or for me[.][13]

Perhaps the most striking feature of Branwell's retelling of the story is the high casualty rate among the successive waves of his toy soldiers. Given an initial set of twelve and then acquiring "another set of the same number" shortly thereafter, when he was seven, the entire twenty-four within "about a year" are "either maimed lost burnt or destroyed by various casualties." The child Branwell then appears to content himself with "a band of Turkish musicians . . . till the summer of AD 1825 when Charlotte and Emily returned from school." The girls' return home was of course occasioned by what soon turned out to be (in May and June 1825, respectively) the fatal illnesses of their older sisters Maria and Elizabeth, which had come on them while they and their younger sisters had been away at school. The "10 months after they had returned" when Branwell remembers himself as soldierless were the period of intensest grieving after the older girls' deaths. As we have noted, Patrick Brontë's gift to his son of the set that became "The Twelve" — actually the third set of a dozen that he had acquired or been given in a two-year period — may have ritually marked the end of the first year of mourning. When Branwell writes his account of the vagaries of his childhood collecting at the end of 1830, when he is thirteen, only two or three soldiers of the third set survive, meaning that there have by now been thirty-three or -four "casualties." He still has his second "set of Turkish musicians" and a "band of Indians." "Here now ends," he intones as if he had been reading the scripture lesson for the day, "the catalogue of soldiers bought by or for me."

As Charlotte tells the story, it is one about Branwell showing his sisters a set of toy soldiers and each of the siblings choosing and naming a favorite. Branwell chronicles the gift of the soldiers by making an exhaustive inventory of them extending over a period of seven years of his young life and over six different sets of toy figures. For the reader interested in what Branwell's account of his acquisition, loss, and destruction of waves of toy soldiers in his childhood may tell us about his own specific experience of the grievous losses he shared with his three surviving sisters, we must draw the story of mourning he may actually be telling out of the implicitness in which it is couched by interpreting it in relation to what we know about the history of the family during the years in question: only in 1825, the family's year of most extreme loss, was he not acquiring or holding a set of toy figures. Two things suggest themselves about Branwell's particular relation to his toys: he wants or needs lots of them, and he is hard on them. There is a kind of austere economy in the set of beloved objects through which Brown imagines Charlotte Brontë perpetuating her mourning for her sisters: the old geography book and the single set of "The Twelve." There is a contrasting note of both extravagance and instability in the sets of beloved objects through which Branwell figures the story of his loss, in which no matter how many sets of soldiers he appears to acquire, the great majority of them become "maimed lost burnt or destroyed." It is important in understanding his story, I believe, not to fail to hear the note of pleasure and triumph, the tone of mock mourning, with which he evokes the destruction of line after line of these figures, alongside (and in a sense inseparable from) the persistent practice of genuine grieving the "catalogue" may also mark. Collecting, destroying, and collecting still more of these figures gives the child—and, by extension, the writer—Branwell his own particular version of the "absurd satisfaction" that Brown attributes to these revivifying mourning practices. Branwell has long been stereotyped as the self-destructive one of the siblings, so early in his life is his association with extravagant need and wasted resources thematized in his own writing and in his writing's place in the family narratives— so much so, I would say, that we might call the particular form of "arrested life" that his writing produces "wasted life." Branwell's mourning practice is a riskier one than the practice that Brown outlines for Charlotte, with its relatively modest supply of "beloved objects." In Branwell's model, in contrast, substantial stores of objects of and for "being wasted" must be apparently endlessly supplied, sacrificed, and resupplied. The peril of making sacrifice (the recurrent wasting of numerous beloved objects) a central part of the mourning practice—as Branwell appears to need to do—is that the wasting principle or function can turn on the self or parts of the self with a devouring ferocity.

As many critics of the Brontës' juvenilia have pointed out, for some years after its beginning, the children maintained a relation of godlike power over their soldier heroes—adapted from their reading of the *Arabian Nights*—in which the children are "genies" (or "genii," in their more Latin form) and the soldiers their human subjects. Charlotte appears to have introduced the concept early on (in 1829, around the time she was turning thirteen and her brother twelve) and Branwell enthusiastically adopted it, denominating himself with boyish arrogance "the chief Genius Branii," as Charlotte is "Genius Talii," Emily "Genius Emmii," and Anne "Genius Annii."[14] The collective role of guiding genii is filled with both grandiosity and self-mockery. The genii make fun of the strange appearance of the soldiers' "boots," which take the form in each case of one outsize black, circular object (they are the little stands on which each soldier has been perched by its manufacturer). The genii sometimes appear in the narratives as vast giants who appear out of nowhere and reorder circumstances like the gods they are. But at other times the genii register the resentment of other beings against these supernatural beings' claim to control the fate of the universe, as in the following much-cited letter to the editor of one of their miniature magazines. The letter reads in full:

> Sir, — it is well known that the Genii have declared that unless they per-form certain arduous duties every year, of a mysterious nature, all the worlds in the firmament will be burnt up, and gathered together in one mighty globe, which will roll in solitary grandeur through the vast wilder-ness of space, inhabited only by the four high princes of the Genii, till time shall be succeeded by Eternity; and the impudence of this is only to be paralleled by another of their assertions, namely, "that by their magic might they can reduce the world to a desert, the purest waters to streams of livid poison, and the clearest lakes to stagnant waters, the pestilential vapours of which shall slay all living creatures, except the blood-thirsty beast of the forest, and the ravenous bird of the rock. But that in the midst of this desolation the palace of the Chief Geni shall rise sparkling in the wilderness, and the horrible howl of their warcry shall spread over the land at morning, at noontide and night; but that they shall have their annual feast over the bones of the dead, and shall yearly rejoice with the joy of victors.["] I think, sir, that the horrible wickedness of this needs no remark, and therefore I haste to subscribe myself, etc.[15]

Alexander comments on the role of the genii in the juvenilia: "Branwell seems to have disliked the role of the Genii and tried to dispose of them by provoking a Young Men's rebellion against their tyranny. Charlotte, however, sees them as an integral part of her creative world."[16] Alexander goes on to note that although the letter is in Charlotte's hand, the "high-flown tone of the writing . . . is that of Branwell," and that Charlotte's "signature has been erased and replaced by "UT"—which has been taken to stand for "Us Two," "implying that Branwell contributed to its composition." Although Alexander does not comment on this point, I take it that in the midst of otherwise universal destruction, the special mention of the survival of the palace of the soi-disant "Chief Geni" (Branwell) is a recognizable touch of Branwell's characteristic mode—simultaneously self-aggrandizing and mock-self-aggrandizing—of representing himself in the early juvenilia.

It is a striking feature of the letter that unlike many other megalomaniacal and mock-megalomaniacal texts, which reserve a place for a presiding deity who is ontologically different and separate from the author—as in Daniel Schreber's writings about the cosmos and its "true" nature in his *Memoirs of my Nervous Illness* (1903)—this collaboration between young Charlotte and Branwell Brontë opens no such gap between the ultimate power in the universe, the "Chief Geni," and any other power, even as it registers both Branwell's claim to universal power and supremacy and his particular *ressentiment* against the ways of "the Genii"—presumably himself most of all. It is perhaps the most extreme statement in Branwell's writing of the particularly violently divided position which is his vis-à-vis the Angrian world and the real universe: he claims sovereign control over it at the same time as he both mocks the claim and resents anyone's making such a claim, himself included. As I shall discuss in more detail below, the homology between Branwell's peculiar way of representing his violently divided attitude toward his own powers of fantasy, imagination, and literary production are in this way strikingly similar to those of Darger, who also appears to imagine himself adrift in an essentially hostile universe in which neither of his fantasized roles—of omnipotence or impotence—brings him any lasting satisfaction, except perhaps the same kind of "absurd satisfaction" that Branwell's comparable means of mourning, and his sisters' less perilous and violent ones, bring them.

For an analysis of the juvenilia such as Brown's that points up its efficacy as a mourning process, the most salient of the genii's magical powers is that of restoring the dead to life, which they repeatedly do in the earlier narratives; one or another of the soldier heroes perishes in combat, and then at battle's end the genii appear and bring him back to life. John MacGregor writes uncomprehendingly of a similar practice in Darger's work: "Darger constantly refers to general or other military personnel as being 'mortally wounded.' These individuals invariably recover, and continue to appear in later battles, suggesting that Darger didn't understand the meaning of the term."[17] More likely, I believe, MacGregor's comment reveals that *he* does not understand that the power of revivifying dead characters may be one of the main plot devices when artists such as Darger or the Brontës spend decades writing "endless stories."

But, to be fair to MacGregor, it may be harder to credit a high level of investment in bringing characters who have died back to life in the work of writers like Darger or Branwell Brontë, who seem possibly to be more interested in depicting mortality in its most morbid and spectacular manifestations than they are in restoring life. We know that as youngsters the Brontës delighted in the "Noctes Ambrosianae" series in *Blackwood's Magazine*, in which the journal's editor and several of its leading contributors (including James Hogg, known as "the Ettrick Shepherd") took on dramatically enhanced writing personae and parodied the bibulous conversations and controversies in which they collectively engaged at Ambrose's Tavern in Edinburgh. The writing of the "Noctes" represented a new model of imaginative and emotional capaciousness in writing in English that was designed to draw in current events, recurrent nightmares, and the grotesque comedy of the body and of personality, along with recognizably romantic and poetic flights of the imagination. One of the recurrent topics of the "Noctes" that combined all of these elements was the social problem of grave robbing as a way of supplying the increasing demand for cadavers for student anatomists to dissect. Criminals who stole recently buried bodies from their coffins were ironically called "resurrectionists," and a part-fearful, part-diabolical fascination with "resurrectionism" manifests itself in some of the Brontës' early juvenilia. For Branwell, one may speculate, the restoring of life to the recently dead may have not seemed an unalloyed good. Just as he could boast of his supreme powers as "Chief Geni" at the same time and in the same document in which he could decry the genii's intolerable arrogance and despotism, so in his writing's fascination or obsession with extreme violence against the body, he shows himself to be both an enthusiastic participant in the genii's powers of restoring life to the dead and a revolted critic of "resurrectionism."

Darger, too, may have had a highly ambivalent attitude toward the possibility of bringing his long-deceased mother back to life. What becomes clear looking back at the history of nineteenth-century "resurrectionist" practices is that by no means were all populations and classes equally susceptible to being snatched from the grave after death. In the United States, for example, the great majority of such robberies victimized the dead of impoverished

African American and recent immigrant communities. The kind of recently immigrated working class into which Darger was born had at the time of his birth a century-long memory of their collective vulnerability to having their graves desecrated and the bodies of their dead stolen. Some of MacGregor's research into Darger's life in the Lincoln Home for Feebleminded Children bring this historical form of terrorizing working-class and underclass populations literally very close to home in Darger's case. Part of the scandal of abuse and neglect at the institution that was exposed by reformers during the time Darger lived there consisted of a resident physician's using organs she had removed from the bodies of recently deceased inmates—and referring by name to the person whose organ she was exhibiting—to teach elementary anatomy to attendants at the asylum.[18] The story in itself does not of course satisfactorily explain, but it provides yet another context in which to try to understand, Darger's fearful fascination in his writing and painting with anatomizing and dissecting children's bodies.

Collecting was clearly a practice that was central to both Branwell Brontë's and Henry Darger's sense of their everyday selves and lives. Yet if imaginarily bringing the dead back to life may have been a practice contaminated for both of them by their impressions or memories of outright abuse of the bodies of the dead, collecting in general may also have become tinged with fear and guilt on the model of the sensational "collecting" that grave robbing and corpse dissection provided them both. Much as Branwell and Charlotte—or, perhaps one should say, Branii and Talii—appear to enjoy their powers of resurrecting their favorite characters from the dead, and central as these powers may have been for them to the practice's efficacy as mourning, after the first few years they stop enacting this power in their writing—and I assume that in this development, as in so many in their writing, Branwell took the lead. Various of The Twelve are killed in one early battle, but, Branwell writes, were "soon made alive by the usual means." Alexander gives a brusque, "do-the-math" kind of account of how the juvenilia had gotten into the business of reviving characters in the first place: "Such resuscitation was [often] necessary in the face of Branwell's overriding desire for frequent battles with limited forces."[19] Yet taking so practical a view of the matter, one is left wondering about the nature of that "overriding" desire of Branwell's. His desire may continue to play an "overriding" role in the juvenilia, but after his early years as the (at least intermittently) self-proclaimed "Chief Geni," it morphs into other forms and practices. After those early years, the genii altogether cease functioning as agents in the siblings' writing and suffer the fate of many such deities in modernity—they live on only as an expletive: the gentlemen in the later writings occasionally swear, unreflectively, "By the Genii!"[20] Perhaps Branwell's "overriding" desire could no longer be satisfied—if it ever had been—by the simple fantasy of undoing mortality by simple reversal. Morbidity itself acquires a kind of compelling animation in his writing, as it does in Darger's work—deadliness "takes on a life of its own," one might paradoxically say, in a way that it does not in Charlotte's writing.

Collecting Spoiled Life

Part of the experience of social death with which Henry Darger struggled throughout his life was his being a member of the massive class of working poor. Doing menial work in hospitals full-time for his entire adult life, he was still barely able to support himself; to augment his insufficient income, he depended on a few key figures in his life, such as his landlord, Nathan Lerner, who did not raise Darger's rent over a period of many years, or the staff of the neighborhood diner, who are said not to have charged him for at least some of his frequent meals there. To my mind, one of the most salient social facts about Darger is that at one time he contemplated getting a dog, but, in consultation with the Lerners, figured out that he could not afford even the very minimal additional expense that he would incur feeding and housing a dog.[21]

The long-term economic unviability of the Brontë family fueled the lifelong pressure each of the children felt from fairly early in life to find some tolerable—ideally, but by no means necessarily, enjoyable—way of earning a living, thereby staving off the collective ruin that must have sometimes seemed inevitable to them. To Branwell, it may have also at least sometimes seemed inevitable that his talent—whether this turned out to be as a writer, painter, musician, or perhaps all three—would bring him (and, by extension, his family) wealth as well as fame. This grandiose expectation, which his family seems to have shared with him for much of his lifetime, appears to have opened some kind of gap in the feedback process that actually prevented him from developing the skills and attitudes that enabled all three of his sisters to become highly accomplished professional authors.

From early childhood, as their "plays" with The Twelve show, all four siblings combined a remarkable rate of productivity (of writing) with a performance of a kind of leisured and privileged literary life in which, for long stretches of time, other activities and responsibilities appear to have taken second or lower place, somewhere below the task of composing Glasstown, Gondal, or Angria. But for Branwell, this dignified leisure was somehow contaminated in a way that it was not for his sisters. He shared with Henry Darger what one might call a "spoiled" identity as both a producer and a collector—"spoiled" in the sense of "contaminated," but, in Darger's case, not in the sense of "indulged," for Darger negotiated throughout his long life the difficult fate of being a collector and proletarian aesthete of sorts with very little in the way of what has come to be called "disposable income." Darger's neighbors saw him picking through their trash cans for the various kinds of objects he collected: broken eyeglasses, bits of string, cast-off coloring books, newspapers, telephone directories; the image has been one of the most widely circulated in the pioneering writing on him and his work. But, as the research of Brooke Davis Anderson into Darger's personal effects, including his bankbooks, have made us aware, Darger did regularly save money—albeit in small amounts—even during the hardest years of the Depression. After steadily accumulating funds for many years, he began to draw on them selectively to cover certain expenses such as (beginning immediately after the Second World War) that of having photographic enlargements of some of his favorite images made so he could trace them into his paintings of the time.[22] Similarly, looking through the books in his personal library, I was struck by the fact that although some of them might have come to him as castoffs from his neighbors or from the hospital where he was working, others he apparently sought out and bought at the used bookstores in his part of town. There is a danger in overemphasizing Darger's trash-can diving to the exclusion of the instances in which we can see him not just accepting what came his way by the humblest routes but at least occasionally seeking out (for example) books for his collection and making choices among them, identifying favorites and adding to the small supply he already possessed of such favorite authors as Dickens, Johanna Spyri, and L. Frank Baum. The danger is in denying him—a proletarian collector—the exercise of the kind of agency of thoughtful and discriminating acquisition so central to the formation of many modern bourgeois subjects, as in young Branwell Brontë's remarkably precise recounting (with respect to numbers and kinds of objects and dates of acquisition) of "the catalogue of soldiers bought by and for" him in childhood. To deny Darger the elements of choice and discrimination that went into the formation of his vision is to impoverish him anew in the way that MacGregor does when he writes: "At no point was his

[Darger's] vision arrived at freely, as a spontaneous, or willed, manifestation of creative choice." MacGregor's own vision of Darger's creativity is itself at least in passing reduced to an astonishingly banal metaphor: "Prolonged exposure to Darger's world, while awakening profound respect for its astonishing intellectual scope, its beauty and aesthetic coherence, also leads unavoidably to the recognition that this endless stream of words and images was born from his mind with the same inevitability and force as the feces thrown off from day to day by his body." [23] If we are unwilling to accept MacGregor's analogy that Darger's work was "thrown off" as shit might be, we must seek further for the nature and meaning of the contamination of the production and collecting processes that Branwell Brontë and Darger both seem to have experienced so intensely.

Elizabeth Gaskell, the Victorian novelist who was a friend of Charlotte Brontë and her first biographer, was clearly disturbed by the collection of miniature books of the Brontës' juvenilia that she was given to inspect as part of her biographical researches: "They are the wildest and most incoherent things," she wrote in a letter to George Smith, Charlotte Brontë's publisher, after making a preliminary examination of them. "They give one the idea of creative power carried to the verge of insanity." [24] But to my knowledge, none of the many critics of Charlotte's juvenilia has questioned either her motivation for writing them or the sanity of her doing so: there seems to be a critical consensus justifying the hours of her youth she spent experimenting with language, character, and situation. The case is different with Branwell. Apparently years after the publication of *The Infernal World of Branwell Brontë*, du Maurier wrote an essay saying that she wished she had taken a more measured and less pathologizing view of his life, but even there she could not forbear observing that she found something fundamentally unbalanced about the sheer amount of writing he did.[25] As in the attributions of some form of compulsive hypergraphia to Darger's writing practice, the very productivity of a certain kind of writer—one who doesn't achieve fame during his lifetime—must be a symptom of psychological or emotional trouble.

Of course, it is not just the sheer amount of the writing (for Charlotte produced at least as many pages of juvenilia as her brother) that seems to impel critics to question the mental balance of figures such as Branwell Brontë and Henry Darger. It is the relative frequency in their writing with which they depict grotesque extremes of behavior, including violent behavior, that makes critics wonder whether the work they are evaluating is crazy or not, or how crazy it is. Counter to the assumption that the high level of violence that manifests itself in these two men's work is a direct indication of an underlying psychological and emotional pathology, I want to take the frequency with which their work reverts to (sometimes extreme) physical violence as an index of how hard each of them had to struggle in and through their work to produce the particular version of "wasted" or "spoiled life" that each of them did in order to attain what was for them the often elusive goal of "absurd satisfaction" that was the only condition that could make their continuing grief over their early losses, and their subsequent respective experiences of social death as adults, bearable. By the same token, I want to consider the frequency of violence in their work to be an index of the frequent and extreme violence that permeated the war cultures that served as primary engines of male socialization and collective male fantasy in Brontë's and Darger's respective societies. Both men may have experienced considerable distress over their failures to live up to the colonializing, war-making male ideal of their times and places. Brontë's inability to leave his childhood home, to hold a job, or to resist "dissipation" all marked him as unfit from an early age; similarly, Darger's discharge from the US Army may have come as a bitter and embarrassing disappointment to a young man who had by his own account long been fascinated with the minutiae of the Civil War.

In considering how their differing experiences of socialization as gendered beings may help one account for the difference between writing like Charlotte's early work, which soon appears to outgrow its concern with extreme violence, and Branwell's and Darger's, which does not, it is probably too easy to relegate an enjoyment of grotesque extremes of behavior, including violent behavior, to the pat category of "a boy thing." If infants of both genders, as Melanie Klein and her disciples have argued,[26] and not just infant males, are commonly subject to feelings of intense rage in which they fantasize invading their mothers' bodies and destroying them from the inside, despoiling them of their biological and sexual "treasures," what about the formation of such modern males as Darger and Branwell Brontë can help us account for their commitment (some would say compulsion) to writing endlessly about physical violence? Brown shows Charlotte Brontë both perpetuating and surviving what began as her overwhelming grief for her oldest sister by discovering or learning how to take an "absurd satisfaction" in a small set of "beloved objects" that she associates with the deceased. With what appear to have been Branwell Brontë's and Darger's rather different experiences of loss and (at least partial) recovery in mind, I want to try to expand Brown's model of mourning in the direction of Klein's discovery of the commonness of infantile rage and rage-driven fantasies of destruction of the body of the beloved (albeit sometimes raged-against) mother. Let us assume that potentially large numbers of people, as infants or small children (or even later, if the fantasies persisted, either consciously or not), have directed fantasies of murderously destructive rage against the body of the mother, and must therefore in some sense mourn the mother—feel the loss (if only imagined), but also feel guilt about the loss as well as fear of retribution for their imaginary attempt to (lay) "waste" the mother's body. So it may not be only those who have actually lost their mothers or siblings as small children, as the Brontës and Darger all did, who feel compelled to mourn—although the actual losses may well have intensified both the painful feelings (of loss, guilt, rage, and fear) and the desire for some relief from them.

I want to think a little about how one aspect of the particular way in which Branwell Brontë's and Henry Darger's experiences were gendered may have complicated or "contaminated" their mourning processes. Different as Darger's social and historical situation was from that of Branwell Brontë, one thing that both men had in common with millions of their male contemporaries is that they had been born into the world of mass armies, for which potentially any male—especially younger men with little or nothing in the way of social privilege—could be conscripted in times of war. This sea change in the circumstances under which males have been socialized was still novel in Branwell's childhood, since it was only in the Napoleonic wars that mass armies had begun to be conscripted and deployed. Surely some of the fixation shown in his writing on the conduct of warfare and, intermittently, on its extreme violence, must be attributed not so much to his personal psychology (or pathology) as to the shock that young men of his generation were still absorbing from the great expansion of the military realm that had just begun in the previous generation.

The US Civil War must have delivered a comparable series of intense shocks to the massive numbers of American men who enlisted or were conscripted into it—shocks that had by no means dissipated as the veterans of the war aged and the United States waged other wars almost continually in the late nineteenth century, first against the American Indians of the West, and then in Cuba and the Philippines. After Darger escaped from the Lincoln Home at the age of seventeen, he appears to have been able to live his entire adult life under the radar of the state and its agencies, except for the time in 1917 when he, then about twenty-five, was drafted into the US Army. Unsurprisingly, given his characteristic behavior—which probably struck army officers as eccentric at best and as evidence of mental instability at worst— he was found unfit for service a short time afterward and was honorably discharged. MacGregor believes that Darger experienced his discharge from the army as traumatic, and that much of the thousands of pages he subsequently wrote about various soldiers of various ranks named "Darger" engaged in endless battle in In the Realms of the Unreal was an attempt to compensate for the insult to him, and to rectify the "error."[27] Since Darger claimed in writing about his earlier life actually to have in many ways enjoyed his life at the Lincoln Home, even calling his situation there "Heaven" in one late piece of writing, he may well have welcomed a return to large-scale institutional life and regimentation that being in the army promised. But I suspect that (just as he appears to have been glad to have escaped from the Lincoln Home, however much he may later have professed to have enjoyed some aspects of institutional life) Darger may have felt relief and satisfaction on being dismissed from the army, at least as much as he may simultaneously have felt rejected and devalued.

Although the Brontës' father, Patrick, was said to have been drawn almost as strongly to a military career as he had been to the clerical life that he subsequently pursued, there is no evidence that Branwell Brontë ever considered enlisting in the military—despite his protracted and, ultimately, interminable vocational crisis between kinds of work as various as professional portrait painter, literary man, live-in tutor, and railway-branch supervisor. Like Darger, he may have written about combat at great length not only because it provided him with some at least partially externalized focus for what may have been a relatively high level of emotional turmoil, but also because it allowed him to connect repeatedly with anxieties he shared with many of his male contemporaries, who either feared conscription or suffered the ill effects of combat—figures with whom these two men might, in their respective contexts, have felt they had little in common.

Here again, although Branwell Brontë and Henry Darger in many ways seem remote from each other's historical and social situations, their respective relationships to and knowledge of warfare and its literature overlaps at what may initially seem a surprising number of points. We find an analogue for Darger's lifelong fascination with the US Civil War in Branwell Brontë's tendency to make civil war the form of large-scale political conflict to which Angrian politics inevitably reverts. The external war that Branwell has Angria fight is also, strangely, part of a conflict that informs Darger's writing as well. Branwell spent much of his youth writing on what the British called the First Ashantee War (which was fought and widely reported in the English-language press in 1824–31). One of the handful of boys' adventure-series books found in Darger's room at the time he vacated it was written by the prototypical British boys' author, G. A. Henty: *By Sheer Pluck: A Tale of the Ashanti War* (1884)—this one the Second War, fought in the 1870s. Far from being remote from the history and myths of warfare in North America, Branwell grew up in a society in which these were still major topics in the leading journals of the day, as well as a major source of didactic material for nursery and schoolroom. His earliest extant writing is a tale about the British invasion of Washington, D.C., in the War of 1814, inspired by an article by "an American subaltern" that he had read in a back issue of *Blackwood's*.[28] A copy of an engraving of Benjamin West's celebrated painting of General James Wolfe's death at the Battle of Quebec hung in Branwell's bedroom during his boyhood.[29] The very fact that the child Charlotte named her chosen soldier "Wellington," England's great national hero, while Branwell called his "Napoleon," England's despised enemy but a hero (at least for a time) to the Irish and other dispossessed peoples in Europe, suggests that Branwell cast himself in the role of antihero and champion of the underdog from the inaugural moment of the children's "plays." Even though he came onto the scene two or three generations after Branwell had, Henry Darger frequently shows signs in both his writing and visual work of an abiding interest in the wars between England and the United States as well as the Napoleonic wars, which by Darger's childhood had taken on an aura of glamour that more recent wars—more clearly remembered and more lethal in their technology and strategies—could not retain.

Branwell begins his account of The Twelves' arrival in West Africa with a description of the location of the country of "Guinea or Ashantee." This he cribs from a geography book—J. Goldsmith's *Grammar of General Geography*, a textbook that the Brontë family owned. (I am assuming that this is not the geography book that Charlotte writes about, since Victor Neufeldt, in a footnote in his edition of Branwell's collected writings, gives 1823 as the publication date of Goldsmith's book,[30] which was therefore almost new at the time Branwell used it, and the book that Patrick Brontë had loaned Maria had been, according to Charlotte, "an hundred and twenty years old" at the time she was writing.) Branwell departs from the textbooks when he claims that "the most likely conjecture" is that "the Ancient British and Gauls" were the first settlers in "this part of Africa," before the arrival of "the natives"—

so that in 1770, when the band of The Twelve set sail from England for the Ashantee lands, they are, in this thoroughly colonialist fantasy, ostensibly returning to an ancestral fatherland rather than launching a hostile invasion and conquest.[31] He sets the scene of The Twelves' arrival in Africa in these words: "For at a time when they [the Ashantees] thought themselves secure from all danger and the Admiration of the whole world a more terrible overthrow and which should more utterly humble them [than] Any other which they had yet experienced was preparing to burst over their unsuspecting heads" (140–41).[32]

The familiar trope of historical irony, the terrific storm just about to "burst over . . . unsuspecting heads," bespeaks the possibility of a kinship between the Brontës' "never-ending story"—especially as this was articulated by Branwell—and Darger's. Darger calls the subject of his grand narrative a "war-storm," conflating the natural with the historical, taking war out of the hands of human beings and at least half-treating it as if it were as much an act of God as a hurricane is. And just as war may strike some people as being as "natural" and inevitable as bad weather, Branwell's just-so story about the Britons and Celts of four thousand years ago (whoever they might have been) having been the "original" inhabitants of West Africa extends backward into history the ostensible naturalness of the British being (back) in West Africa. Darger performs a comparable kind of historical sleight of hand when he has the "slaves" over whom is fought the long, tragic, massively destructive civil war of which he writes all appear to be white children.

Massacre Culture

The most striking resemblance between Branwell Brontë's and Henry Darger's imaginary worlds lies in the central part played in both by the extreme physical violence of war, complete with massacres and atrocities. One of the most telling differences between their two bodies of work lies in the way that each of them treats race as a significant (or insignificant) feature in their respective chronicles of social and political conflict. Branwell may (absurdly) invite his readers to imagine that the British were in West Africa long before the "natives" were, but, unlike Darger, he does not generally banish racial difference to the far margins of his work. Although much of the strife he depicts in his narratives is internecine and even fraternal, he does not disguise the fact that many of the larger-scale conflicts he depicts take the form of race war. Indeed, he undoes any boundary we might imagine maintaining between the fraternal (supposedly personal and small-scale) and racial (supposedly large-scale) axes of his stories by having the Duke of Welling-ton, early in the saga, adopt into his own royal family the fiercest of the young Ashantee princes, Quashia Quamina, whom he rears as one of his own sons. Much—although by no means all—of the most spectacular vio-lence depicted in Branwell's writings is projected onto the figure of Quashia. Take, for example, the Massacre of Dongola, a supposedly crucial event in the Duke of Zamorna's "First War . . . For the purpose of clearing the Ashan-tees From the rightful Territory of Angria," written by the seventeen-year-old Branwell in late 1834, in the persona of "Henry Hastings the Poet of Angria": [33]

> As I held up my face to the sky to catch a breath of air in the crowd I saw something which made me shut my eyes and turn my head down that mo-ment. From a pole which had been an inn sign and which stuck out of the Gable of a House beside me Hung suspended almost over my head a raw and bloody corpse the skin flayed off the gore blackened over the carcase and the throat severed with a ghastly gash stretching from ear to ear. The men before me were marched forward and I could now see all the mar-ket place around us and There Nailed upon close rows of wooden crosses reared up along the sides of the forts and houses I beheld more than 200 Dead Bodies of men with the scalps torn from their heads their mouths skewered up with knives and the dried gore hanging in black lines from their livid sides In the midst of the area. A heap of several hundred car-cases their heads chopped of[f] and piled at random among them and all burnt and blacked by a fire which had been kindled round them diffused through the air a dreadfully singed and putrid smell. [34]

Zamorna calls on his troops to counter massacre with race war: "By the spirits of my soldiers who have been martyred for my country . . . I swear to you that I will not sheath this sword till I sheath it in the heart of an Ashantee that I will not lay it by till . . . there is not one Accursed savage left alive. you must spare nothing Angrians slay them whenever wherever however you can find them slay the men slay the women slay the children give no quarter But exterminate from the earth the whole d—d race of Ashantees." [35] Zamorna appeals to his soldiers to avenge Angria on every Ashantee person, but he also specifically blames his own foster brother: "Quashia has thus treated your fellow soldiers and companions." Writing years later, in the latter part of 1845 (he was then twenty-eight), Branwell has his hero Alexander Percy accuse Quashia of all the evil deeds his own fellow Angrians are having urged on them by their king and commander in the passages above: "brutalities, torturings—[be]headings—hangings, roastings, [flayings] alive—burning man woman and child."[36] Quashia is described in the same context as having been in his life "a slave . . . a slave driver . . . a slave owner, and after wards a pirate captain" (3:446). Quashia, the so-called Demoniacal Black who has been taken into the heart of Angria's ruling family, is depicted as eventually avenging himself (and his people?) on the Duke of Zamorna by dragging the Duke's firstborn son, Ernest Edward "Fitzarthur" Wellesley, from the arms of his nurse and executing him by driving a hot iron rod into the small boy's eyes.[37]

Readers coming to such scenes as these with some knowledge of Darger's *In the Realms of the Unreal* may be shocked to discover passages in the Brontë juvenilia that share some of the most disturbing features of the frequent scenes of battlefield carnage and massacre in Darger's work. The blurring of war with religion and feelings of religious indignation and righteousness around issues of alleged martyrdom (Branwell's city of Dongola is itself spoken of as "martyred" [2:302]; hundreds of Angrian soldiers have not just been massacred there but have literally been crucified), the extensive descriptions of bodily violation in mass atrocities, the inclusion of children as objects of massacre by the Angrian commander ("slay the children give no quarter") or the kind of vicious atrocity allegedly committed by Quashia Quamina on the person of Zamora's little son—are similar to parts of Darger's writing and painting.

When Branwell describes a fierce battle that takes place beside a river, which soon becomes so densely packed with the bodies of the slain that the surviving troops are able to march over the mass of corpses to the other side, a reader may well think he is simply overdoing the grotesquerie, even for scenes that can be as exorbitantly violent as those of combat in wartime. But, as Neufeldt notes, "grotesque as this episode seems," it appears to be based on a similar incident reported in a March 1825 article in *Blackwood's Magazine* titled "The Subaltern—A Journal of the Peninsular Campaign" (the Brontës' Twelve are supposed to be arriving to colonize West Africa immediately after having served in Wellington's peninsular campaign against Bonaparte).[38] Similarly, Darger's scenes of mass carnage inflicted on his child slaves may strike the reader as certain evidence of pathology on his part, but, as with the bloody and revolting military scenes the Brontë children read in *Blackwood's*, one has not far to seek for historical analogues to the horrific scenes depicted in *In the Realms of the Unreal*. Readers today may feel skeptical about and even suspicious of what may well strike them as the frequent rank sentimentality of Darger's writing. But consider this example, chosen almost at random: "Many of the wounded soldiers as well as the unfortunate refugees I knew well in person and these gave me greetings as good friends, but Good God it was nothing but a sad handshake and flowing tears. . . . It would be utterly impossible to write without becoming a part of this sad story myself." [39] Born in 1892, Darger turned twelve in 1904 and came of legal age in 1913. Rather than seeing the frequent oscillations in his work between sadistic and sentimental responses to the horrors he depicts as merely a personal pathology, the student of Darger's work should be mindful that he had been born into a particular historical and political situation in which massacre and lynching were everyday occurrences, frequently and extensively reported in the newspapers, and that responses that may seem grossly sentimental to readers today were widely understood a hundred years ago as expressing strong feelings of sadness and regret (and perhaps political despair) over the cruelty inflicted on the victim.

The vocabulary of sentimentalism indeed provided one of the few alternatives to professing to find one's feelings in the wake of especially calamitous and deplorable happenings to be "inexpressible." When the US government ethnologist James Mooney composed his official report on the Wounded Knee Massacre in the year Darger was born, he quotes one of the party who had buried the frozen bodies of the several hundred Minneconjou Lakota men, women, and children shot down by soldiers of the US Army: "It was a thing to melt the heart of a man, if it was of stone, to see those little children, with their bodies shot to pieces, thrown naked into the pit." [40] There are thousands of sentences like this in Darger's writing. At the beginning of the twenty-first century, it is probably hard for many readers not to feel repelled by what may seem to be an obscene juxtaposition of appalling violence and excessive sentimentality, but our almost automatic repulsion should not blind us to the political critique of cruelty and injustice, and the appeal to justice and humanity, being made by this kind of juxtaposition, even if it is not the way we ourselves would make such an appeal (or even if it is not the kind of appeal—given its universalizing assumptions about justice and humanity—that we would make at all).

Around the time Mooney was writing his report, Oscar Wilde was subverting the Victorian cult of the dying little girl (in which Darger, an ardent fan of Stowe's Little Eva, was to become so heavily invested) with such quips as: "One must have a heart of stone to read the Death of Little Nell without laughing." The very idea may have shocked many of Darger's contemporaries, but not Darger himself, for he often shows his Glandelinian villains laughing at the piteous and horrific deaths of their child victims—as often as he shows their Angelinian allies weeping over their dead bodies or graves. Similarly, if Darger's apparent fixation on the image of a little girl being strangled and eviscerated strikes some readers today as certain evidence that (to put it crudely) he must have had the mind of a pedophile serial killer, the reader should stop and consider how openly reports and images of lynching—the vigilante execution of African Americans by hanging, often accompanied with torture before hanging and mutilation of the corpse after death—were circulated in Darger's childhood and youth in the United States in the opening decades of the twentieth century. Torture, strangling, and the mutilation of corpses were not merely gothic fantasies in Darger's America, they were events of which probably few children could have been entirely unaware. White-supremacist violence against African Americans reached an all-time high at the end of the First World War, and by no means was this violence confined to the South: so-called race riots in which many more blacks than whites were maimed and killed, and entire black neighborhoods were burned and looted, occurred in record numbers in what was known as the Red Summer of 1919, in Darger's hometown of Chicago as well as in St. Louis, Tulsa, and more than a dozen other American cities.

Neither did the Brontës have to range as far afield as Africa for memories of massacre and political violence. Veterans of the Peterloo massacre and the Luddite uprisings were still living in substantial numbers in the Yorkshire of their youth—people who vividly remembered demonstrating and sometimes rebelling against the conditions of their employment and being beaten and shot at for doing so. There is a recurrent character in the Glasstown-Angria chronicles—a figure in Northangerland's retinue, a grizzled old man called Pigtail—one of whose nefarious specialties is the abduction and murder of children. It would be too easy to attribute his origins only to the imaginary boogeyman who haunts so many nurseries and fairy tales of the grimmer variety. Pigtail may embody a memory, however vicarious, of the fact—chilling then as now, especially to children—that there were significant numbers of child laborers who fell in the onslaughts against the rebelling workers of the early battles against industrialization. Since it was not at all uncommon in Branwell Brontë's lifetime for boys to join the British Navy at the age of nine, military personnel who were in fact children were inevitably involved in both inflicting and suffering extreme violence.

In observing that Branwell Brontë and Henry Darger grew up in worlds in which extreme political violence was a not infrequent occurrence, I want to oppose the notion that the violence of their respective bodies of writing can be taken simply as symptomatic of personal disturbance on their parts. But I do not mean to suggest that narratives of atrocity do not also in a sense carry on a life of their own, at the level of both highbrow historical narrative and popular folk memory. As Union sympathizers fled the Battle of Bull Run, shocked to see their side defeated in the first big engagement of the war, one of the first stories to attain wide circulation in the North was that Louisiana Zouaves, intoxicated with bloodlust and victory, had decapitated a number of wounded Union soldiers and kicked the heads around the battlefield. There were many atrocities committed in the course of the war, and no doubt some of them went unreported. But this reported one, at least, seems not to have actually ever taken place, but instead to be a kind of group fantasy expressing grief, horror, and fear of much further mass violence and its (to this point) largely unforeseen consequences.

The Erotics of Spoiled, Wasted Lives

Oscar Wilde professed to be unable to suppress laughter as he read of the death of Little Nell in one of Darger's favorite books, The Old Curiosity Shop. MacGregor imagines Darger engaging in what is in our own time a much more scandalous activity, and that is becoming sexually aroused as he wrote about the strangling or evisceration of the little girl slaves of In the Realms. MacGregor quotes not one of these scenes of terrible violence but another kind of scene, in which a child is depicted being "made happy" by the painless (indeed, intensely pleasurable) "injection" that one of the guardian Blengin serpents makes into the child's body: "They [the needle-like tubes in Blengins' mouths] are sharp but also hollow, and at times a fluid of a very sweet smell comes from them. Those are the lances with which if pierced into the blood veins of a little girl or boy causes him or her [to feel] the strange happiness as soon as the fluid is injected."[41] And he comments: "This passage provides one of the few indications we have in the writings that Darger had experience both of masturbation and of orgasm," but he does not explain how this little fantasy about injecting a fluid "indicat[e]s" things about Darger's alleged sexual experience. The "needle-like tubes" and the "sweet-smell[ing]" fluid they emit might signify infantile memories of the pleasures of breastfeeding and (in aggressive and angry fantasy, at least) the guilty thrill of biting the breast or piercing or injuring it by other means, rather than necessarily betokening postpubescent experiences of masturbation and ejaculation on Darger's part, as MacGregor wants them to do. MacGregor appears to take Darger at his writing's and drawing's word (so to speak) about not having any understanding about physical sexual difference or about "penetration"; I believe Darger both knew and did not know these allegedly "fundamental facts" about human sexuality.[42] "What is rape?" Penrod, the main boy character in In the Realms asks at one point. "According to the dictionary," one of the Vivian sisters quickly responds, "it means to undress a girl and cut her open to see the insides."[43] I have trouble imagining that Darger never opened a real dictionary himself and looked up the word "rape" and read a dictionary definition of it—not, of course, the one given by little Joice Vivian. Even if the "real" dictionary definition were euphemistic, and it may well have been, it would in some sense have contradicted this childish "definition."

"While Darger was clearly aware of right and wrong, it is doubtful that he had any understanding of the sexual nature of his sadistic fantasies," MacGregor writes in the course of another discussion of what Darger did or did not "know" or understand about sexual matters.[44] He immediately adds, in a footnote, "This is not to imply, paradoxically, that these same fantasies did not lead on occasion to sexual arousal and orgasm."[45] One page later, in a related footnote, he admits, "I am aware that I am assuming a connection between Darger's sadistic fantasies and masturbation in the absence of evidence."[46]

I am troubled by the tendency among some commentators on Darger's psychology, including MacGregor, to assume a hard-and-fast (so to speak) connection between scenes of brutal violence and a "normal" (allegedly typical of adult males) type of sexual response: arousal, increasing sexual excitement, orgasm—in, as MacGregor admits, "the absence of evidence." There may be a greater lack of connection among sadistic fantasy, sexual arousal, masturbation, and orgasm in Darger's case than MacGregor seems to allow for. MacGregor readily recognizes the self-annulling circularity of the reasoning of the physician who officially admitted the twelve-year-old Darger to the Lincoln Home, as this registers itself on the admissions form, in the answers provided by the admitting physician, presumably in consultation with Darger's father:

> At what age and in what manner was any peculiarity first manifested?
> Self abuse from six years.
> State any peculiar habits the child may have.
> Self abuse.
> Is the child given to self abuse or has it ever been?
> Yes.
> What cause has been assigned for its mental deficiency?
> Self abuse.
> Is it considered congenital or acquired?
> Acquired.
> Is the child insane, or has it been pronounced insane by the physician?
> Yes.[47]

No evidence of "insanity" except "self abuse" is adduced on the form. Although we do know on the evidence of his work that Darger was fascinated by or obsessed with violence against children, especially the strangulation and evisceration of little girls, it does not seem clear to me that we can stably attach an adult male and sadistic sexuality to this recurrent scene. Rather, he may well at some moments and in some ways have identified with the aggressors in this kind of scene, but it seems to me that he also might have identified with the victims and, perhaps more than with either of these, with the narrator, describer, chronicler, or observer of the scene (these latter roles are by no means necessarily all the same). No one of these positions, I believe, can necessarily be assumed to be the one that Darger assumed (often and regularly) in response to the violence recurrently depicted in his work.

The entry for "sadism," with fifty-four references listed, is one of the longest in the index to MacGregor's study of Darger. Strikingly, in a study of an immense body of work that is as obsessed with experiences of pain and suffering and ostensible sacrifice as Darger's is, there is not a single entry for "masochism" or even for "sadomasochism" — as if "sadism" in and of itself were a sufficient explanatory category for what MacGregor himself shows to be the immensely complex affective charge of Darger's work. Some of the other longest entries in MacGregor's index are those for "murder" (also fifty-four references), "rage" (fifty-one), and "aggression" (forty-four). Although MacGregor claims in his book to have rethought his earlier sensationally pathologizing characterization of Darger as "psychologically . . . a serial killer," his supposedly considered version of Darger is still one in which sadism, murderous rage, and aggression are given the foreground and countertendencies to these affects and behaviors are hardly even given names.[48]

In the way that MacGregor seems to feel compelled to corral Darger's work into a few channels marked "sadism," "rage," "aggression," he is participating in a long-established medical practice of reducing people to familiar (and often highly stigmatizing) categories. As we have seen, as a boy of twelve, Darger had experienced the violence of being categorized as insane for the sole reason that he practiced so-called self-abuse. In our own time, a psychiatrist's diagnosis of sadism brings along with it certain assumptions about the primacy of rage and aggression in the subject's psychological makeup. A hundred years ago, a person who was convicted of masturbating was also suspected of being insane or epileptic, and all three of these conditions were routinely confused with one another. After establishing to the admitting physician's satisfaction that Darger was insane and masturbated, and in some sense *was* insane because he masturbated—or was it that he masturbated because he was insane?—the admissions form of the Lincoln Asylum continues: "Were there ever any cases of epilepsy or insanity in the family of the father?" "No." "In the family of the mother?" "No. Grandmother on mother's side had fainting spells."[49]

Although this may seem to be only more fishing for "hereditary" disorders, readers versed in the history of sexuality will recognize that it is actually an extension of the preceding questions about self-abuse, for in the early twentieth century and for some time before, epilepsy, insanity, and masturbation had all been posited as each other's causes, effects, and symptoms. "Noncongenital" or "acquired" epilepsy, like insanity, was widely considered to be an effect of excessive masturbation. Parents tended to try to keep epilepsy in their children secret, partly because of the potential sexual shame or deviance associated with it. This opinion had hardly changed at all over the previous century. In speculating why Branwell Brontë, the only son in his large family, was educated entirely at home and never sent away to school, as all his sisters had been, du Maurier speculates about whether he may have been subject to epilepsy and kept "close to home" by his father for that reason (the hypothesis also helps make sense of his tendency to "fits," with particular kinds of attendant cries and breathing, that Branwell is reported as having had at various crises in his life).[50] One of the central events in the legend of Branwell Brontë is that his young life was ruined when he was fired from his tutoring position in the Robinson household for having fallen in love with or having become sexually involved with the wife of his employer. Making a careful review of the sequence of events surrounding Branwell's dismissal leads du Maurier to argue that the serious "misbehavior" took place not in relation to Mrs. Robinson, who was traveling with her husband at the time, but more likely with Branwell's pupil, their adolescent son Edmund.[51] If Branwell had been kept at home most of his life because of concern (or shame) over his epilepsy, some vague reputation as a somehow sexually excessive or perverse young man may have preceded him into his relations with the Robinson family and with people outside his family in general. His Angrian world is so intensely male homosocial that it would be surprising if there were not moments of high homoerotic romance in it, as when Hector Montmorency, the young Alexander Percy's "familiar," publicly breaks off with him with a half-ironic citation of David's remark to Jonathan: "thy love to me was wonderful[,] passing the love of woman."[52]

In reading Branwell's writings, much of the time it is quite hard to know where to imagine locating their author's sexual arousal or pleasure. As is the case with Darger's work, the potential subject of sexuality often seems to be in several different possible places at once, in a not altogether legible configuration. The paucity of signs of what might be taken to be erotic pleasure in Branwell's work may lead us to pause over a tiny undated drawing of his with particular interest and curiosity. The editor of his published visual work, Jane Sellars titles the drawing *Figure Studies* and describes it in these words: "To the left is an embracing couple and to the right a group of three men lounging on the ground, all of them with their legs crossed loosely above the ankle. Two of them, facing in opposite directions, smoke pipes and the third man appears to be masturbating. Long-barrelled guns lie on the ground. It is possible that the men are smoking opium and that all of them are indulging in masturbation."[53] "Although these pencil sketches . . . are tiny," Sellars writes, "they are worth noting as they contain images of decadent behavior, which, bearing in mind the speculation about Branwell's own conduct at this period, may have some significance" (what that significance might be, she does not say). Although calling masturbation and the smoking of opium "decadent behavior" sounds more like someone writing in 1895 than in 1995, I take Sellars's point. Although rightly observing that given the different directions in which they are facing, the other two figures whose genitals and right hands are concealed from the spectator may also be masturbating, Sellars fails to consider (and consequently misses much of the potential charm of the composition) that the three figures may simply represent the same masturbating man seen from three perspectives, from only one of which is his sexual activity visible to an observer. That makes the drawing more of a joke with a punch line: we can look at a man simply sitting outdoors peaceably smoking his pipe, regard him from a second perspective and see the same sight, and then from a third perspective realize that the man may be masturbating as well. It seems easy to me to imagine this image as highly expressive of an erotic desire of Branwell's—one for solitude outdoors, given that he shared a closet-size nursery with his three sisters and a bedroom with his father during childhood, and had to share the bedroom with his father again as an adult after he was sent home in disgrace from the Robinsons. Maybe Sellars is right and the pipe is full of opium—getting high, getting aroused, and masturbating outdoors in splendid isolation and privacy (at least from two of three possible directions) might well seem an appealing pastime, at least in fantasy, to someone living in a domestic environment such as Branwell's that was almost totally lacking in private space.

One may then understand this image as a kind of witty comment on Brontë's part on his general lack of domestic privacy in the crowded little Haworth parsonage he occupied with his family almost his entire life. But one may also interpret the significance of the drawing as possessing some talismanic force for him, as a visual articulation of something he knows, thinks, or feels (we may imagine) but never articulates in the masses of writing he produced: masturbating in a relaxed and unhurried fashion, somewhere outdoors where no one else is around is a reliable pleasure, or the thought of it is. Several commentators have noticed what may be a similar kind of disjunction between what Darger appears to have felt he could draw and what he felt he could articulate verbally when they observe that for all the regularity with which he draws his "denuded" girls with boys' genitals, nowhere in his writing does he ever mention their "unusual" genitalia.

But in interpreting the tiny drawing of Branwell's in this pastoral fashion, I may be overlooking or underestimating the degree to which it may have been designed to shock and dismay some potential viewers; it may be a sign not so much of the desire for privacy and pleasure on the part of someone in Branwell's position as it is of such a figure's contempt for the social niceties of "relaxing outdoors"—and therefore fueled by anger as much as it may have been by desire. At recurrent moments in Branwell's writing, as here in his drawing, many valences of the erotic seem spoiled in advance of their possible enjoyment by anyone. Darger's work also often seems to participate to some degree in this pervasive atmosphere of "prespoiled" erotic plea-sure. Branwell's writing is particularly articulate about this; when, for ex-ample, his "Rogue," Alexander Percy, Earl of Northangerland, is stirring up his lieutenants to join him in betraying his king and son-in-law, Zamorna, and fomenting war to the death in Angria, he inveighs against Zamorna and Zamorna's rule in tones of biblical bombast that evoke a kind of absolute contamination: "The Hideous Mass of corruption which though dead yet speaketh and though abhorred by all yet rules over all." [54] One readily recog-nizable echo sounds in the middle of the sentence: "which though dead yet speaketh" is a quote from Saint Paul in Hebrews 11:4, on how God looked favorably on the sacrifice of Abel and unfavorably on that of Cain; according to Saint Paul, God's approval of Abel means that though "he [be] dead" he still "speaketh" through his good actions and God's continuing sanction-ing of him and them. In the sibling rivalry that fueled the Angrian chronicle (itself the product of a remarkable and remarkably sustained instance of sibling collaboration-cum-rivalry between Charlotte and Branwell), both ruler and rebel, Zamorna and Northangerland, partake of more than a bit of (Byron's as well as the Book of Genesis's and Saint Paul's) Cain; only North-angerland at his most dastardly and treasonous can make Zamorna seem Abel-like, even temporarily. I imagine Northangerland realizing, if only for an instant, as he indulges in this characteristic patch of rhetorical overkill, that "The Hideous Mass of corruption" against which he is advocating re-volt is not just his king, Zamorna, but, as characters in science fiction movies often used to say, "is bigger than the both of us."

Like the implacable fury that fuels Darger's doomed search for his lost photo clipped from a newspaper, a fury which he sometimes "feels" but which also sometimes becomes "bigger" even than he and any lost (or ab-ducted) little girl could be, so that he (and his "endless story") at times become quite dissociated from it, "The Hideous Mass of corruption" that both haunts and impels Branwell's version of Angria defies definite iden-tification or specification. Perhaps the theorist who has come nearest to illuminating the murky reaches where such things dwell (but where they refuse to stay put) has been Eric Santner, in his 1996 study of Schreber's *Memoirs of My Nervous Illness*, in which Santner (I think very suggestively) re-lates the "psychotic" operations of Schreber's text to what were Schreber's excruciating experience of (in Walter Benjamin's phrase) "*something rotten in the law.*" Santner explains: "What manifests itself as the law's inner decay is the fact that rule of law is, in the final analysis, without ultimate justification or legitimation, that the very space of juridical reason within which the rule of law obtains is established and sustained by a dimension of force and violence that, as it were, holds the place of those missing foundations." "At its foundation," Santner goes on, "the rule of law is sustained not by reason alone but also by the force/violence of a tautologous enunciation—'The law is the law!'—which is for Benjamin the source of chronic institutional disequilibrium and degeneration."[55] I understand both Branwell Brontë's and Henry Darger's apparent (and shared) predilection for scenes of gruesome and grotesque mortality as the strong desire they also shared to expose and explore what they perceived as the rottenness of the rule of cosmic law in their respective worlds. Both artists at times seem consumed by their similar visions of the ungrounded and ungroundable foulness that is all that ultimately establishes the law the supposed foundation of the worlds each of them makes.

The language in which both Branwell Brontë's and Darger's respective causes of death are commonly given partakes of the fantasy of pervasive corruption—something fundamentally rotten about things at their very core—that was central to either artist's output. "Consumption" covered a multitude of ills in nineteenth-century medicine. For a long time, later readers took the allegation that all the Brontë siblings except Charlotte had died of "consumption" to mean simply that they had died of what came to be called tuberculosis. But more recent work in the social history of medicine and epidemiology has made us realize that "consumption" does not necessarily translate into a single disease or illness. One reads nowadays, for example, that the two eldest Brontë daughters died of malnutrition as a consequence of what we would probably tend to call the "Dickensian," but might as well call the "Brontëan," conditions that had prevailed at the clergymen's daughters' boarding school to which they had been sent. The reports of the causes of Branwell's death are the most complex and ambiguous of the entire family: some of the alleged causes are essentially moralistic ("dissipation" and so on), others point to "addiction" (supposedly to alcohol and opium), while other sources invoke what turns out to be the blanket term, "consumption," leaving the uninformed reader to equate this with tuberculosis. The actual cause entered in the official record of his death is "marasmus," "wasting disease," which (like "consumption") can mean a wide range of symptoms and disorders. It often means "the effects of chronic malnutrition" and long meant with respect to infants and the old something almost as vague as "failure to thrive." "Emaciation" or "loss of flesh" also appear as synonyms of "marasmus" in old dictionaries. The term has also had a long career as a metaphor for lamenting one's own degraded state, as when Samuel Beckett's Murphy cries: "I am half dead with abuse and exposure, I am in a marasmus" (see *Murphy*, chapter 8).

According to his death certificate, Henry Darger died of arteriosclerotic heart disease.[56] MacGregor quotes Nathan Lerner's last memories of Darger, of a very old man sitting in the nursing home where he died "almost catatonic."[57] I assume by "catatonic," Lerner meant to suggest that Darger seemed to him to be extremely uncomprehending or uncommunicative. But according to the *Oxford English Dictionary*, the actual meaning of "catatonic" is "a form of insanity, characterized by epilepsy"—in other words, like the epilepsy that may have caused the Brontë family to keep Branwell at home until he was grown, or the "insanity" with which Darger was diagnosed (and for which he was confined) for masturbating in childhood, "catatonic" is in essence a stigmatizing term, of the kind that blighted (spoiled)—and perhaps also helped energize—the lives of both these men.

The heaps of paper, art materials, and detritus of numerous kinds—as well as his vast books of writings and equally vast book of illustrations—that were found in Darger's room after ill health had finally forced him to vacate it attest to the other side of the kind of "wasted" or "spoiled" life that had fueled his and Branwell Brontë's respective lifelong creative projects—the other side from the "wasting" diagnosis of "marasmus." Branwell Brontë and Henry Darger were, for all their very real differences, both the kind of men that their respective societies might well have professed to find "unbalanced"—or, in the more lurid juridical and pseudo-diagnostic vocabulary of the *fin de siècle*, "degenerate" and even "perverted" and "decadent." They had been in somewhat different ways spoiled as boys and both had (in a rich and highly ironic sense of the term) wasted their lives. The almost intolerable truth that makes both their bodies of work still such unwelcome—and indeed in most ways unreceived—"news" is that the rottenness of much of what they have to show us may be neither an effect nor a symptom of their personal histories or psychologies, but a fundamental and constitutive element of their—and our—worlds.

Chapter 3

ABDUCTION,

ADOPTION, APPROPRIATION

DARGER AND THE EARLY NEWSPAPER COMIC

STRIP; OR, READING AROUND IN THE RUINS

OF A PROLETARIAN PUBLIC SPHERE

> These interminable stories are
> indeed like an immense system of
> burrowings in the world of fantasy
> and imagination made . . . by ano-
> nymity itself. In these illustrated
> palimpsests there are traced not
> only our jokes and our business
> but our dreams.
> —William Bolitho, "Comic Strip,"
> *Camera Obscura*

In order to adapt William Bolitho's description of the early newspaper comic strip to make it fit Darger's work, we need only recognize that in Darger's case, not only are "these interminable stories . . . indeed like an immense system of burrowings," but they are also an immense system of borrowings as well. My desire in these pages is to demonstrate, in what I believe is Darger's by no means anomalous case, how thoroughly his world was not really a private or secret one, particular or unique to him (no matter how clandestine his characteristic mode of working may have been), as much as it was in many ways a public one composed of the myriad elements scavenged during a lifetime of reading and viewing and collecting images and narratives and rhetorics from a bewildering array of sources, from *Don Quixote* to *Mutt and Jeff*. The comparably wide range of intense and varied responses that readers and viewers—especially, but not only, poets, painters, musicians, choreographers, and other artists—have to his work suggests that even though Darger may have kept it to himself during his lifetime, his is a truly popular art, in both its formation and its effects.

In his work as a visual artist, Darger started out collaging photographs of children and soldiers cut out of newspapers and magazines and embellishing them with his own drawing and writing. Then, for most of his career, he traced the images of the children he drew, scavenging them from comic strips, coloring books, and newspaper and magazine advertisements, organizing them into large groups in landscapes of his own devising. Students of his writing have been quick to discover in it an analogous practice of lifting language. Stealing, raiding, ransacking, poaching, kidnapping—all these and other ostensibly forbidden actions characterize Darger's artistic modus operandi, giving his work its edge, its way of continually producing the "cheap thrills" of plundering the stores of others to supply oneself and one's gang with (real or metaphorical) food and fuel and, beyond that, to supply oneself and others with that sheer excess that we call "fun."

In Darger's work, all this plundering is carried on in the name of the possibility that individuals and an entire class of people ("child slaves") can escape the bitter condition of servitude in which they live (which extends to the threat, and sometimes the execution, en masse, of torture and murder) and at least eventually satisfy the intense yearning for freedom that they feel. In imagining the conditions under which this might be possible, Darger seems to concur with many of his (and our) contemporaries that waging and winning a war is ultimately the only way of securing freedom for oneself and one's fellows—and the more massive its scale, in terms of both the numbers of people involved and the duration of the conflict, and the more destructive its effects, the better. Through the medium of the narrative of a protracted war fought through dozens of battles involving millions of soldiers, civilians, and refugees, Darger produces a field in which the stories he tells of the sufferings and triumphs of his heroines, the Vivian Girls, and their child allies take on the contours of a struggle for freedom that often fails disastrously and, even when it succeeds, must wrest what freedom it can, and wrest it repeatedly, from an extremely hostile world pervaded in most places and times by an apparently implacable evil.

What are we to make of the apparent homology that Darger's work sets

up between his method of producing art—radical and continual appropriation—and his model of human freedom as having to be wrested, only
with great difficulty and through extreme violence, from the unalterably evil
masses who would deprive us of it? "Plagiarism," which is Darger's preferred
means of producing his writing, is a term that entered the English language
in the early seventeenth century, derived from the Latin noun *plagiarus*, to de-
note not "one who appropriates the writing of another," the current meaning of plagiarist, but "one who abducts the child or slave of another." The
Oxford English Dictionary gives "kidnapper" as a synonym, but, interestingly,
"kidnapper" actually replaced "plagiarist" in its initial sense only toward
the end of the eighteenth century: to "kidnap," again according to the *Oxford
English Dictionary*, "originally [meant] to steal or carry off (children or others)
in order to provide servants or laborers for the American plantations." So
the kind of story Darger tells—about the interminable struggles of a mass
of child slaves to free themselves, against overwhelming odds—has its lin-
guistic and terminological roots in a mass of narratives from early modernity (the seventeenth century and after) about the abduction of large numbers of children and others to serve as slave laborers forced to build the New
World and the institutions of its European settlers under desperate and often
torturous conditions. Darger's most characteristic mode of composition,
plagiarism, enacts a similar, if relatively harmless, form of abduction—in
this case, of words and images. But in studying his work, I am struck by the
regularity with which its appropriated words and images recur in scenes of
the abduction and violation of children, as though the borrowed forms and
materials could never be quite effectively purged of or detached from the
sometimes extreme violence associated with the appropriation of children
as slave laborers.

Darger "abducts" words and images in order to tell endless stories of capture in warfare, detention, rescue, and escape. These stories are focused on
children, as both captives and rescuers. In Darger's work, as well as in the
larger body of literary and mass-culture narratives on which he models his
work, stories about little girls who are taken captive by squads of malevo-
lent men and rescued by gangs of other little girls, sometimes with the aid
of benevolent adult male allies, segue readily enough into stories about un-
conventional family formations in which children and certain adults form
something more like sibling bonds than parent-child ones. Complementary to the many tales of abduction in Darger's work are the many tales of
this somewhat unusual form of adoption, in which siblings adopt additional

siblings, sometimes without regard to the age of the adoptee. At one point the Vivian Girls set about adopting—that is, persuading their parents to adopt—the girls' own adult guardian, Captain Jack Evans (they somehow require a guardian despite having both parents living, which one may take as a sign of their royal status).

Darger and William Schloeder, the friend of his youth, made some attempts to adopt a child when they were themselves young men, but their efforts were unsuccessful. In our own time, when adoption by male couples is receiving widespread attention, we may anachronistically assume that the rejection of Darger and Schloeder's bid to adopt was in some sense fueled by what we would call homophobia. But recent histories of adoption in the United States make us realize that in the first three decades of the twentieth century, so much emphasis was placed on whether the prospective female parent possessed genuine maternity as the indispensable characteristic couples needed to qualify as adoptive parents that a male couple might just not register as a genuine possibility at the time. Indeed, the thinking of the time seems so wedded to the notion that femininity combined with maternity was essential to proper child rearing that adoption by single women and female couples reached an unprecedented height in these very decades, and unconventional-looking "parent couples" were for awhile increasingly common—as long as each set of parents contained at least one woman. Although the records show that successful bids for adoption were made by various women in conjunction with (for example) a father-in-law (in the case of one young widow), a hired man (in the case of an unmarried woman farmer), and a bachelor brother (in the case of "two maiden sisters"), I see no sign of successful bids being placed by a male couple. Rejected as an adoptive parent, Darger began to write about himself and his buddy Schloeder as leaders of "the Gemini," an avowed child-protection league. It is unclear from the archive whether this was just a compensatory fiction on Darger's part or the two (and perhaps other) men actually convened themselves into some kind of organization, but (as I shall discuss below) a surviving document or two suggest that the latter possibility is a real one.

Popular attitudes toward adoption—especially the adoption of children of Darger's class, those of the urban poor—had changed drastically in the time between Darger's birth in 1892 and 1909, when he finally left the asylum where he spent his adolescence. Darger became a half-orphan when his mother died in childbirth before he was four, and effectively a full orphan at eight, when his father ceased to be able to take care of him. Although orphaned middle-class children of several generations before Darger's could hope to be placed in homes where their individuality and spontaneity were respected and encouraged, poor children had often been indentured as long-term servants or field hands and sometimes treated little, if any, better than slaves. In Darger's childhood, even those displaced children who were not legally indentured were often expected to take on heavy workloads to "earn their keep." In the decades leading up to Darger's birth, "orphan trains" became the most widespread means of placing orphaned or unwanted children of the poor in large cities—a practice pioneered by the philanthropist and reformer Charles Loring Brace and the influential Children's Aid Society he founded. In New York City, for example, in the late nineteenth century and the early twentieth, tens of thousands of children were "rescued" (some of them in fact were kidnapped from intact but impoverished families) from the poor parts of the city and sent West "for their own good." Advertisements were placed in trade papers and farm journals in the hinterlands, announcing when an orphan train was scheduled to stop at a given junction. While farmers crowded around, feeling the muscles and checking out the dental health of potential selections as they might at a livestock fair, some of the children would demonstrate their good will and biddability by singing songs and reciting poems. Sentiment probably played an insignificant part in most of these "adoptions." Children who were not selected were bundled back onto the train to try their luck again at the next stop.

Large orphanages with more or less permanent child populations of the kind that Darger had inhabited were under steady attack at the time. Progressive child savers were devoted to making orphanages only temporary refuges for most children, getting them back out into the broader population as soon as possible. Strong anti-Catholic feeling among many US reformers and their constituencies fueled some of this opposition: mass orphanages under monastic supervision and strict religious discipline were viewed as a peculiarly Roman Catholic (and therefore unsatisfactory) way of dealing with long-standing problems of orphanhood and child homelessness. In fact, an established discourse at the turn of the last century sharply criticized the established institution of the large orphanage for turning out exactly the monklike, unsocialized, beaten-down, robotic "nobody" kind of personality that Darger probably struck those few of his contemporaries who noticed him as possessing. Since the thousands of children in the Lincoln Home were considered feebleminded or otherwise deficient, potential adoptive parents were unlikely to consider adopting them, given the highly eugenicist thinking of the time, which continued to associate degeneracy and depravity with physical and mental handicaps. During his years at the asylum, which was located in rural Illinois, Darger became one of the big boys who were placed as summer laborers with farmers in the area. He wrote in his autobiography that he hated this (it is apparently the main reason he finally fled the asylum, where in some ways he enjoyed living), not because of the hard work he was required to do as a temporary farm worker but because being "placed out" fundamentally disrupted his daily routine, to which he was deeply attached.

John MacGregor's interpretation of Darger's fascination with adopting a girl suggests a direction we might take in our thinking about Darger's investment in this somewhat uncanny idea of little girls' successfully appropriating the heroic male role while, in most ways, remaining little girls (albeit girls with what appear to be male genitals). "We know that Darger desired to adopt a little girl and at several points in *The Realms* he claims to have done so," MacGregor writes. "But, paradoxically, his deeper desire seems to have been a wish that he might be adopted by little girls."[1] The desire to be adopted by a gang of little girls that one could in turn adopt oneself was a wish that was unlikely to come true in Darger's society, but his writing and painting both grant and withhold from him fulfillment of the wish. In the course of his narratives, the Vivian sisters extend a web of adoption widely, but they never speak of adopting any of the many figures they encounter named Darger. Perhaps for them to do so would have been redundant, since he and they already shared the textual space he had created in *In the Realms*, where they could engage in endless relations of mutual adoption and appropriation.

Since Darger's mother had died when he was still a toddler and he lost (to adoption), at the same time, the newborn sister to whom his mother had just given birth (and would lose in adolescence his last remaining close relative, his father), it is easy to understand why fantasies of orphanhood and adoption were especially highly charged for Darger. But in looking at the kinds of materials he collected, read, and collaged into his work, what has surprised me is the remarkable frequency with which orphanhood, kidnapping, and adoption recur as leading narrative motifs in the saga-style narratives of both elite and mass cultures in the early decades of the twentieth century—from the theatrical adaptations (and early films) of work by Charles Dickens and Harriet Beecher Stowe and their successor sentimental novelists to the *Oz* books, the newspaper headlines of Darger's early youth, and many of the most popular early newspaper comic strips of the 1920s and 1930s. Although one may think of adoption as what usually happens to children in orphanages, and abduction or kidnapping (especially for ransom) as something that was likely to happen only to children in intact families, and probably especially in affluent families, the abduction of orphans—the kidnapping of children who had no family to defend them from abduction or to attempt to track them after they had been abducted—was a problem that received very widespread publicity in early twentieth-century media.

In 1904, the year that Darger entered the asylum at the age of twelve, there occurred the widely publicized scandal of what the historian Linda Gordon calls "the great Arizona orphan abduction." A group of nuns belonging to the order of the Sisters of Charity set out from New York with about forty orphans (mostly of Irish extraction, aged three to five) whom they intended to place in Arizona with Roman Catholic Mexican families. When local Anglos got wind of the plan, they seized the arriving orphans and nearly lynched the band of nuns for intending to place white children with families of an allegedly "inferior" race. (The nuns may have been surprised to hear self-proclaimed whites claiming the kids as their own—the children of indigent Irish families back in the poorest neighborhoods of New York City hardly counted as "white" in those days). Various of the white protestors "adopted" the children themselves, and the Arizona State courts supported their "rescue" of the orphans. When the Foundlings society with which the nuns were associated took the case all the way to the US Supreme Court, the Court declined to hear it, claiming lack of jurisdiction. Preserving racial segregation and white supremacy trumped considerations of religion. Controversial as the case was, white majority opinion seemed satisfied with the legal outcome.[2]

Between the time of the "great Arizona orphan abduction" and the even more highly sensationalized Lindbergh child abduction case of the late 1920s (which is also to say, between the time Darger himself entered an orphanage and the time his writing of In the Realms was well under way), newspaper comic strips developed into one of the most widely disseminated forms of the much expanded mass media of the time. Given the high level of feeling in the United States about changes in child-placement practices and policy, and the recognition of the news media that stories about such controversies sold millions of copies of papers, it is unsurprising that in such newly and massively popular comic strips as Gasoline Alley, Dick Tracy, Little Orphan Annie, and Little Annie Rooney, Darger and his contemporaries encountered an endless web of narratives in which often volatile relations among orphans, official caretakers, foster or adoptive parents, kidnappers, and policemen held center stage for weeks and months at a time. Over the years, Darger cut favorite comic strips of his out of the daily paper, including many install-ments of *Little Annie Rooney*, and pasted them into scrapbooks. At different times and sometimes repeatedly, each of these strips provided yet another slow-moving but intermittently emotionally intense narrative that may well have stimulated and confirmed Darger's sense of himself as an orphan who had in a sense been abducted as a child and now, as an adult, deeply desired to adopt a child—and (as MacGregor has suggested) may have even more strongly (if more or less unconsciously) desired to be "adopted" not just by a child but specifically by a gang of little girls.

My contention is that if Darger and his desires seem bizarre to many people, that may be not so much because the desires are in themselves espe-cially weird but because Darger (inadvertently or not) left an extraordinarily elaborate and extensive record of his intimate desires and fantasies. Follow-ing the work of Oskar Negt and Alexander Kluge, among others, I want to ar-gue that far from being merely personal, private, or secret, fantasy draws its elements from public life and in various ways returns these elements, often in transformed condition, for further circulation among the public. Negt and Kluge want to restore to fantasy some of its character as productive labor, in the face of the long-established common-sense dichotomy between real productive labor and the ostensibly lazy daydreaming and so-called mental masturbation that fantasy allegedly amounts to. They understand the pro-duction and circulation of fantasy as an indispensable feature of the making of modern proletarian public spheres. They also point out that we end up being appropriated by the very objects that we appropriate in fantasy—that fantasy is indeed a process of getting "carried away" by the objects of our fantasies. For them, Darger's wish to be adopted by a gang of little girls would be only an inevitable effect of his wish to adopt a little girl, and vice versa.[3]

Negt and Kluge are concerned with how the increasing commodification of our fantasies shuts down some of the most psychically and potentially po-litically productive work that fantasy (for example, various forms of utopian fantasy) has done in modernity. To my mind, Darger's work represents an ex-treme example of this dynamic because of the paradoxical way in which he is both heavily constrained by and in other ways able to escape and oppose—by offering a countermodel to—the increasing commodification of pleasure in the United States and other affluent societies in the course of the twentieth century. Through his writing and painting, Darger devised ways of allowing the objects of his fantasies to appropriate him that provided him—and potentially his readers—some satisfaction of his desire to be adopted by a gang of little girls. This virtual reciprocity had been at least partially enabled by commodities (children's book series, newspaper comic strips, Catholic devotional materials, and so on) but was by no means entirely dependent on them. Darger's work suggests that he successfully passed through a prolonged phase of falling in love with his fantasy objects and entered an equally prolonged phase of establishing something like stable affective relations with them. His development of his remarkable artistic abilities as an image designer and colorist in addition to his vast writing project suggests that he found ways of renewing and extending his creativity well into later middle age (in itself a notable accomplishment).

Although Darger may never have felt even the desire for the kind of self-conscious awareness of himself as a worker in at least potential solidarity with other workers that would seem to underlie Negt and Kluge's notion of what a worker or proletarian must be, I would contend that Darger's work does evince a powerful desire for there to continue to be, and come to be more of, a number of the proletarian public spheres that were in formation (and in contest) during his lifetime. So far, the bulk of analytical attention to the emergence of such spheres in Darger's lifetime has gone to early cinema—the nickelodeons with their low admission prices, their location in relatively downscale urban neighborhoods, and proletarian fare, including sensational (and often faked) news footage, title-bout boxing matches, zaftig women exposing cleavage and legs, heavy practical jokes, and a full range of ethnic-stereotype "humor."[4] The parallel realm of the newspaper comic strip, which was coming into enormous popularity during the same decades that the cinema was (roughly 1890 to 1925), has received relatively little attention as a site for such analysis. But although Darger mentions films and their plots and stars only very sporadically—just often enough for readers to perceive that he had seen films, at least in his earlier days, and been impressed by at least a few of them—we know him to have been a life-long aficionado and collector of newspaper comic strips.

When Darger read the comics pages of the *Chicago Daily News* in the decades after his return to the city in late adolescence, what kind of world did he encounter? The single term most often associated with the first several decades of comic strips is "anarchic": an uncontainable energy circulates through the doings and mishaps of such lowlife characters as the Yellow Kid, a bald, nightgown-clad street urchin, and Happy Hooligan, a good-hearted but often misunderstood and mistreated hobo. "Hooligan" was a new word in 1900 when the strip bearing that character's name began to appear, and it meant "young street rough" or "gang member," with an obvious nod toward the Irish-American ethnicity of the presumed miscreant. A century later, it's hard to imagine a popular comic strip in US newspapers being called *Happy Gang Member*. The very idea that a gangster could be characteristically happy bespeaks a degree of interested sympathy in the rowdy street life of the times and its denizens that is greater than we are used to seeing today. But, especially for readers of roughly Darger's age who themselves grew up in synch with the first generation of rough, slap-happy comic strips, a way of reading and understanding the comics as a place where raffish characters habitually gave the finger to their straitlaced, disapproving neighbors had become well established by the time that the comics themselves became less street-friendly.

By peering into the archive it is possible to get a few glimpses of the young Henry Darger as a denizen of this early twentieth-century world of proletarian leisure, someone who enjoyed amusement parks, outdoor food vendors, ragtime music, and silent-film comedy. As he later describes in his autobiographical writings, Darger was accompanied on many of his forays into this world by William Schloeder, whom he met and befriended around 1910, a year or two after his return to Chicago, when he was seventeen or eighteen. Four photographs of Darger are in existence, and two of them show him with Schloeder in the kind of jocose photographers' setups in which young people out for a good time in the early twentieth century had their pictures taken. In his autobiography, Darger recalls insisting on treating Schloeder when the two men went out to amusements on the weekend. Schloeder and his family appear to have emigrated from Luxembourg, and since Darger's father and uncle had emigrated from Germany, Schloeder's European origins and foreign accent may have been part of his appeal for Darger. Schloeder moved with his sisters to the Chicago suburbs in the mid-1940s, and Darger probably saw less of him after that. Schloeder and one sister moved to San Antonio in 1956; Darger continued to write him — in care of his sister, because (according to Darger) Schloeder could not read or write English.

There are recurring and magniloquent references in *In the Realms* to the activities of the Gemini and to the heroic roles that Darger and Schloeder play in the group. We might assume that this was entirely Darger's fantasy were it not for a few pages of documents in the Darger archive that suggest that the group may have actually met for a time and, even though the name "the Gemini" suggests a twosome (twins), it may even have had more than two members. MacGregor describes a letter to Darger signed by a Thomas A. Newsome (and not in Darger's handwriting) which refers to a "Supreme Person" who is identified as head of the Gemini; another unknown person and alleged member of the group called "our beloved Rodney Graves"; and the recipient's (presumably Darger's) "Lincoln friends," suggesting that the Gemini may have started among Darger and a group of his fellow inmates at the asylum for feeble-minded children that Darger had escaped from in 1909. The letter goes on to direct its recipient to appear at the office of Thomas Wentworth, in Evanston, to pick up a sealed "envelope bearing the name of Rodney Graves," and enjoining complete secrecy about the matter.[5] MacGregor, who has thoroughly researched Darger's early environment, can make nothing of the letter. What the particularly tense mixture of fiction and reality around the doings of "the Gemini" and of Darger and Schloeder does suggest to MacGregor is that Schloeder is by far the most likely candidate to have been shown some of Darger's work, as the only other person who appears to have participated with Darger in some of the activities—trying to adopt a child, and declaring themselves a "child protection agency" when they proved unable to do so—that seem related to some of the continuing concerns of In the Realms. If, as Darger mentions, Schloeder could not read English, he could not have read Darger's writing, but the artist could have shown him some of his early collages and drawings of figures in the narrative. Perhaps more important, Darger may have discussed his work with Schloeder and did draw his friend into some of the activities, such as the doings of "the Gemini," where the line between "the realms of the real" and "the unreal" fade to invisibility—or at least, at this distance, to illegibility. And Schloeder does sometimes appear as a character   predictably, a confederate of Darger's—in In the Realms.

In the years following Darger's and Schloeder's failed attempt to adopt a child, during which Darger continued to work on his tales of the abduction and rescue of children in wartime, newspaper comic strips took up the topics of orphanhood, kidnapping, and fosterage with remarkable frequency. In one of the most popular strips of the time, Frank King's Gasoline Alley, a fat young bachelor auto mechanic named Walt is astonished to find a week-old baby boy abandoned on his doorstep (this is depicted in the strip published on February 14, 1921). For its first several years, the strip had concerned itself almost entirely with a group of men in a small Midwestern town and their tinkering with their cars—cars were still novelties for many Americans around 1920, and many readers who had just begun to own or aspired to own one avidly followed *Gasoline Alley*. At first, Walt tends to treat the baby like a malfunctioning little auto, but with the help of the neighbor ladies, a series of nursemaids, and the discovery in himself of previously unsuspected depths of feelings for the foundling, he soon becomes proficient at infant care. The strip depicts Walt's "parent's progress" in loving detail week by week and, eventually, year by year: the infant "Skeezix" famously grows up in the strip in real time, contracting the usual childhood illnesses, serving in the army in the Second World War, and making Walt a foster grandpa twice, in 1945 and 1949 (the strip even celebrated Skeezix's seventy-fifth birthday in 1996). In the early years, there are inevitably questions about who the baby's real parents are and even some skirmishing over custody, but overall the strip presents Walt's experience of single parenthood circa 1920 as a benign and, indeed, generally pastoral one.

How can Darger be faulted (in retrospect) for being unrealistic about his prospects as an adoptive parent, when even iconic tough guy Dick Tracy was shown participating in a cycle of highly emotionally charged narratives about the abduction and adoption of children in order to launch the popular strip in which he appeared? *Dick Tracy* had been running in newspapers for only a few months (beginning in October 1931) when Charles and Anne Morrow Lindbergh's two-year-old son was kidnapped, on March 1, 1932. Unlike the Lindbergh case, which tragically climaxed in the discovery of the dead body of the abducted child, Tracy gave his readers all the narrative satisfactions that were getting frustrated by the "real" case: he recovered "the Waldorf Baby," restored it to its parents, and struck its kidnapper such a blow that it propelled him through a locked door. During that same inaugural year, Tracy adopted a reformed boy criminal who renamed himself "Dick Tracy, Junior" and became the detective's diminutive other self. (Even the street bum Happy Hooligan, who was always shown wearing a tin can on his head as a hat, eventually acquired a son, "Little Happy," who sported a smaller tin can.)

The steadfastness through tribulation of some of his child scout characters in *In the Realms of the Unreal*, and especially the secret-sibling ties that sometimes emerge between various of them and some of the other most appealing characters, bespeak Darger's absorption in this particular body of modern mythology. Amid the social upheavals of the early twentieth-century

United States, such characters continued to struggle on in some of the comic strips Darger clipped out, pasted into scrapbooks, and traced and collaged into his paintings, such as his favorite (and, in his work, much traced and transferred) *Little Annie Rooney*, launched early in the new year of 1927—the response of the King Features Syndicate (and the Hearst corporation) to the great success of *Little Orphan Annie*, which had been launched in mid-1925 by the rival syndicate at the *Chicago Tribune*. Both names were already familiar to readers: "Orphan Annie" from a figure in James Whitcomb Riley's 1885 poem "Little Orphant Annie," and "Little Annie Rooney" as the heroine—a young domestic paragon—of an 1890s popular song of that title and then, in 1925, a popular movie in which then-superstar Mary Pickford (aged thirty-one) played a twelve-year-old tomgirl gang leader of the urban slums. Claudia Nelson, in her recent study of the depiction of adoption in American popular writing from 1850 to 1929, uses what she sees as the striking distance between Riley's "Little Orphan Annie" of the 1880s and Gray's comic-strip character of that name of the 1920s, to demonstrate how thinking about orphanhood and adoption had changed during that time. Riley's Annie is based on a "bound" (indentured) girl who actually worked in his family's house as a young maid of all work, who told his children bedtime stories ("the goblin'll get you / Ef you don't watch out!") about how people who are unkind to orphans (like herself) are punished by ghosts. She is an underclass part of the household, a kind of lower appendage and domestic convenience, colorfully humorous. Forty years later, Gray's Orphan Annie is a full-fledged melodrama heroine, adored by her adoptive father, envied and disliked by her adoptive mother, the focus of endless plots to displace her from and reinstate her as the treasurechild of a vastly rich and powerful family.[6]

As the foster daughter of Daddy Warbucks, Little Orphan Annie was recurrently the object of nefarious kidnapping schemes. Darger's apparently strong preference for Little Annie Rooney over Orphan Annie may be a key to one aspect of his taste and sensibility when it came to comic-strip orphan narrative, for Annie Rooney is a crucially important source of visual, and perhaps for narrative, material in his work. According to the comic-strip historian Maurice Horn, Annie Rooney, in sharp contrast with the "feisty, belligerent moppet" who is Orphan Annie, is a sweet and rather passive girl whose attempts to escape the orphanage and its cruel female superintendent and her crack team of runaway-child trackers seem inevitably to end in failure (fig. 6). At one point, Rooney appears to find her Daddy Warbucks in

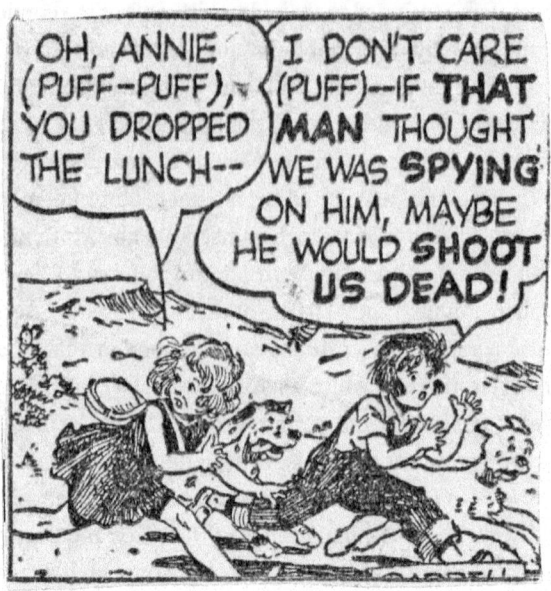

FIGURE 6. Darrell McClure (1903–87). "Little Annie Rooney."
Newspaper clipping from the collection of Henry Darger.
Collection American Folk Art Museum, New York. Gift of
Kiyoko Lerner © Kiyoko Lerner 2003. Photographed by
Gavin Ashworth, New York.

the figure of a kind and elderly millionaire named Mr. Bullion, but he soon loses his wealth and disappears from her life. *Little Orphan Annie* is clearly a crash course in surviving the Depression by maximizing a certain familiar version of self-reliance; to this all-American fantasy, *Little Annie Rooney* provides a clear alternative of a somewhat odd kind—one that stresses (in both senses of the term) the extreme vulnerability of its child heroine. The French critic Jean-Claude Romer has called *Little Annie Rooney* an unlikely combination of the Comtesse de Ségur (who wrote cloyingly sweet stories about girls for the nineteenth-century nursery) and the Marquis de Sade.[7] Readers who have come up with similarly "unlikely" combinations to characterize Darger's work may be surprised to learn that Darger encountered just such work in the pages of the local daily newspaper, year in and year out.[8]

Through repeatedly tracing the figure of its heroine into his drawings and paintings, Darger brought *Little Annie Rooney* directly into his visual art (fig. 7

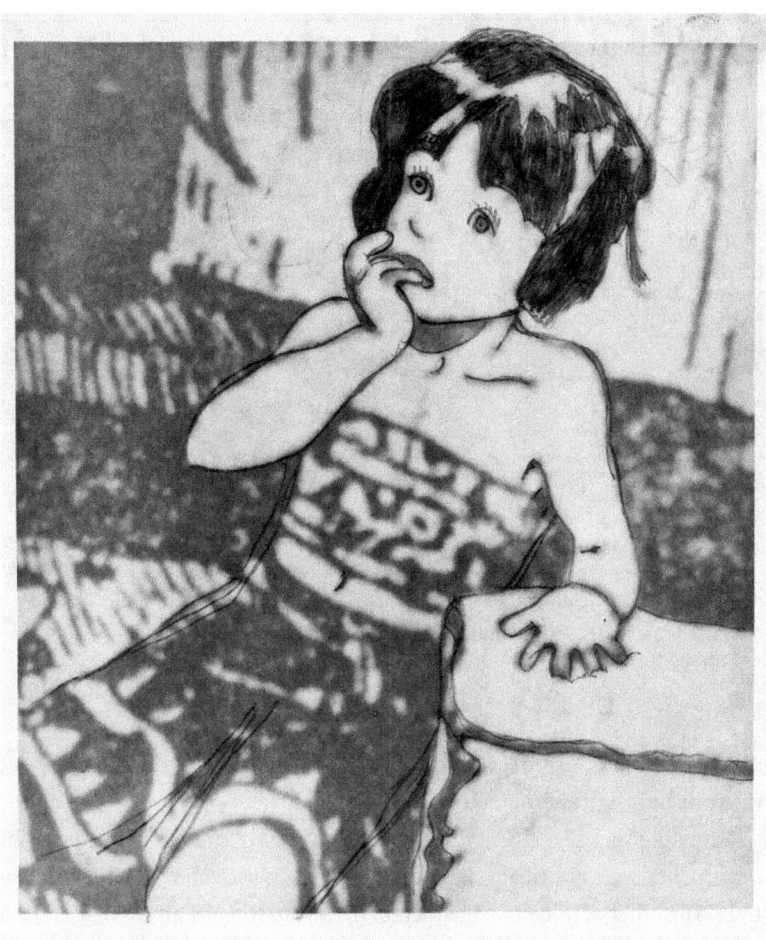

FIGURE 7. Darrell McClure. "Little Annie Rooney." Newspaper clipping altered by Darger from the collection of Henry Darger. Collection American Folk Art Museum, New York. Gift of Kiyoko Lerner © Kiyoko Lerner 2003. Photographed by Gavin Ashworth, New York.

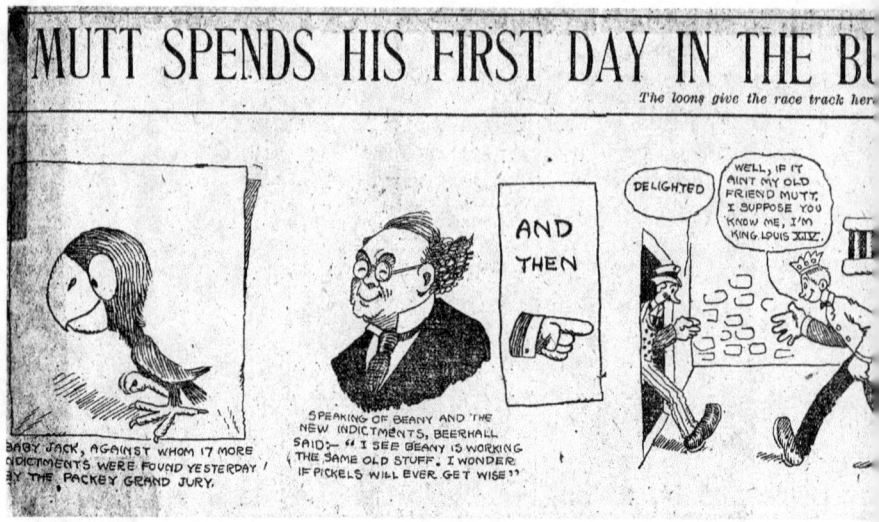

FIGURE 8. Bud Fisher (1885–1954). "Mutt and Jeff: Mutt Spends His First Day in the Bughouse and Is Welcomed by All the Bugs" (1909). Courtesy of the Billy Ireland Cartoon Library, The Ohio State University, Columbus, Ohio.

shows Darger in the process of transferring an image of Little Annie Rooney into one of his girl heroines).

Annie Rooney is a character who is relentlessly "traced" and tracked by the cruel mistress of the orphanage where Annie lives, and her hired detectives. The other comic-strip characters that Darger made an explicit and extensive presence in his own work are Bud Fisher's Mutt and Jeff, but in their case, he includes them only in his writing, never in his visual work. MacGregor points out that Darger may have started reading *Mutt and Jeff* soon after his return to Chicago in 1909, after himself escaping from the Lincoln Home, and he may or may not have been aware of the back story from 1908 about Mutt and Jeff's having escaped from an asylum to form their unlikely and highly ineffective but nonetheless permanent partnership. MacGregor also mentions that given the enormous popularity of the strip at the time, and the distinctly odd appearance when they were together of Schloeder, who was quite tall, and Darger, who was quite short, the two were an example of a type then universally known as a "Mutt and Jeff"[9] (fig. 8).

Since for most readers it is their appearance that makes them such a memorable duo—tall, rangy Mutt alongside short little Jeff—it is especially

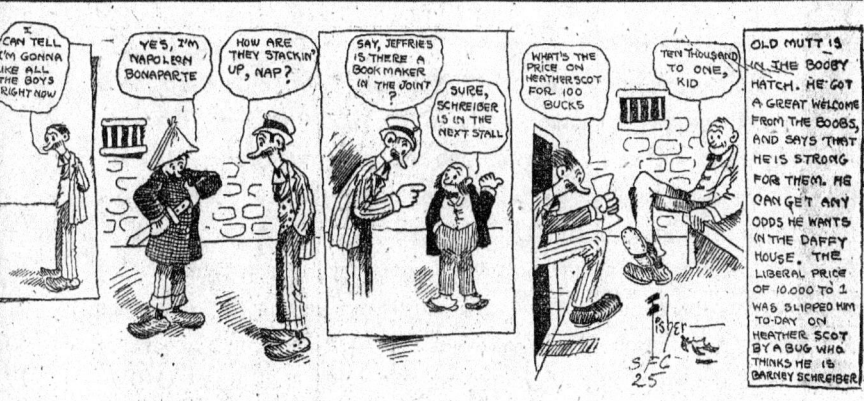

striking that although they "appear" numerous times in the written text of
In the Realms, Darger did not depict them in any of his visual work. In focus-
ing on *Mutt and Jeff,* Darger was hybridizing his writing with one of the oldest
strips in the newspaper; indeed, historians of the funny papers consider the
strip, which began running in 1907, to have been the first successful multi-
frame comic strip in a newspaper. When, a year or two earlier, Fisher had
first proposed drawing a daily strip of several successive panels each, his
editor had allegedly nixed the project on the grounds that not only would it
take up too much space, but it would also conflict with newspaper readers'
well-developed habit of reading column-wise—vertically, not horizontally.
The strong horizontal thrust of Darger's visual compositions may derive in
part from the model that Fisher and his successors established in the comic
strips in the second decade of the twentieth century, with a grammar of the
visual that extended much farther horizontally than it did vertically. Darger's
innovation was to monumentalize the shape.

Mutt and Jeff, with its endless recycling of con tricks, "nuthouses," and
horse races, punctuated on a nearly daily basis with regular swift blows to
the head, is very much part of the proletarian world in which comic strips of

the first generation were set. It is easy to imagine that the knockabout world of the early comics page was more congenial to Darger than the bourgeois ideals that predominated in other sections of the newspaper, such as the society page. Like several strips of its kind, *Mutt and Jeff* initially appeared on the relatively raffish sports page. For its first year, the strip was entitled *A. Mutt* and was concerned only with "the tall one," a would-be grifter who spent every day trying to scrape together a little money so he could place a bet at the tracks (hence its placement on the sports page). Then Mutt acquired Jeff, his inseparable sidekick and foil of the seventy-four years that the strip continued to run, and the two entered the realm of the proverbial. Confined to an insane asylum for a while (after having been jailed briefly) for petty theft and related malfeasances, Mutt encounters a series of other men who believe they are Shakespeare, Louis XIV, Napoleon, and various Civil War generals. Out of this group emerges a short, bald, imperturbable man who claims to be "Jeffries"—Jim Jeffries, then heavyweight champion of the world, the so-called Great White Hope who came out of retirement to box (and lose to) the African American champion Jack Johnson. When the presidential election rolls around in the fall of 1908, the asylum's Bughouse Party nominate Mutt as their candidate and Jeff as his running mate. When a volume of the strips appeared in 1910, Jeff assumed full costar status for the first time in the book's title, *The Mutt and Jeff Cartoons*. It was not until Fisher brought the strip to a new syndicate, in September 1916, that Jeff's name finally became part of the strip's title.[10]

"Short and tall" was only the tip of the semiotic iceberg that formed under and around the phrase "Mutt and Jeff" during Darger's lifetime. "Mutt and Jeff" were the poor man's Don Quixote and Sancho Panza, partners in another indissoluble, if sometimes volatile, friendship in which violence played a significant role. The *Oxford English Dictionary* definitely takes a jaundiced view of the pair, defining "Mutt and Jeff" as "a pair of people having widely divergent characteristics, especially dramatically different heights; a pair of stupid, comically ill-matched men." Some historians of comic strips hear the "mutt," the mongrel, in Mutt's name; others hear "Muttonhead," meaning "Stupid." The dictionary may be right in saying that people have used the phrase "Mutt and Jeff" to mean "a pair of stupid . . . men," but in that case people have erred, for it is Mutt, the would-be crafty one, who is recognizably stupid. Jeff may be crazy, and he certainly is naive and literal minded, but he is not stupid.

The characters of Mutt and Jeff undergo a remarkable moral metamorphosis in Darger's hands. For him, both men are thoroughly—and fascinatingly—evil and, far from being stupid, are all too capable in their careers as spies and *agents provocateurs* for the Glandelinian forces. MacGregor sees a specially strong bond of authorial identification in Darger's revision of little Jeff, whom he makes "the ringleader" of all the Glandelinian spies, "a very bad man," who has, with Mutt's aid, "always made big money, and even made suckers of many Glandelinian generals." To this already hefty catalogue of sins and crimes, Darger's narrator adds that little Jeff "has also a reputation of being a great assassin of children."[11]

The comics historian Robert Harvey writes: "We laughed at them [Mutt and Jeff] both, but we merely tolerated Mutt and his schemes; we loved little Jeff." Harvey sees the "unwittingly victorious" outcomes of Jeff's bumbling survival of all the "traps or pitfalls" Mutt sets for him as vindicating a belief that "the benevolent nature of humankind . . . triumphs eventually over its baser instincts in the long, long run." Harvey quotes *Mutt and Jeff's* creator, Bud Fisher, asserting in a 1920 interview that although almost everyone else prefers Jeff, he favors Mutt—apparently on the contrarian principle that otherwise "almost every person in the world is for the little guy against the big one." Fisher says he has always considered Mutt "my pal and friend" because (supposedly unlike Jeff) he "is trying, and making mistakes, just like the rest of us, and he is a rough worker at times."[12]

The cult of the little man against the big in the 1920s was no guarantee against the nascent fascism of the time, which became increasingly invested in discovering more ways in which masses of "little men" could overcome their ostensible alienation from at least some "big men." When Darger looked at Bud Fisher's drawings of supposedly lovable "little Jeff" and saw a figure of "big money" and treacherous espionage, with at least a "reputation" for assassinating children, and made him a recurrent character in In *the Realms*, what might that tell us about the way Darger exemplifies a way of reading newspaper comic strips—a way that has left few other traces—other than the self-flattering mainstream ones of taking Mutt and Jeff as simply "a pair of stupid men," or either of them as simply some kind of lowly good guy? Harvey speaks of human benevolence overcoming "baser instincts" not just in the long run but "in the long, long run." As Darger performed the lifelong labor of giving In *the Realms of the Unreal* the long, long unfolding that his favorite comic strips had, he can be seen—among the other things he may have been doing—as having mounted a counterattack against a tendency in his society to read the funny papers without sufficient emotional commitment and daring. In his revision of Mutt and Jeff, especially "little Jeff," into thoroughly evil men, and capping off the catalogue of Jeff's sins with that of serial child murder, Darger gives his readers a glimpse into the heart and mind of a man who would, on the basis of what readers might assume from his work were his fantasy predilections, be posthumously and sensationalistically suspected of child murder himself. Through the massive webs of narrative of child abduction that circulated around and through Darger's work and the world from which he derived it, at least the "reputation" (to use Darger's term for Jeff) for committing such chilling crimes came unfairly to be lodged against Darger himself.

Darger's radical recasting of Bud Fisher's dweebish Jeff into a master manipulator of men and an assassin of children gives us a rare glimpse into one reader's fantasy use of a character in a newspaper comic strip that was read by millions on a daily basis for much of the twentieth century. Raised with the perception that Mutt and Jeff are harmless and corny, many of us may initially have a hard time seeing what about the pair could have sparked visions of terror and mayhem in Darger's imagination. But Gilbert Seldes—his nearly exact contemporary who was a distinguished cultural critic and the pioneering champion of American lowbrow culture—had no trouble seeing the dark and demonic possibilities that Mutt and Jeff embodied for their early readers in his classic essay on "The 'Vulgar' Comic Strip" in The Seven Lively Arts. For Seldes, Mutt is a rare creation insofar as he is a genuine American picaro and rogue, an amoral risk taker for whom there is "nothing too dishonest" or underhanded to try. "When nearly everything else in the same newspapers is given over to sentimentality and affected girl-worship," Seldes writes, "it is notable that the comic strip remains grotesque and harsh and careless." What America considers to be its serious art and writing, he argues in this 1924 essay, it largely condemns to being middlebrow and earnest. Only the most raffish of its comic strip heroes are allowed to explore, on a daily and immensely public basis, the "more violent, more dishonest" sides of life. As Seldes sees them, Mutt and Jeff, along with a few fellow bums and rogues from other early strips such as Happy Hooligan and Barney Google, bear the burden of representing to a mass readership the possibility of an energetically proletarian way of life, of not respecting "law, order, the rights of property, the sanctity of money, the romance of marriage, and all the other foundations of American life."[13]

The newspaper comics pages would undergo a sea change less than a decade after Seldes wrote his prescient appreciation of the enormous "vulgar" energies and lowlife graces of life on the street, at the tracks, in the taverns and flophouses of the early twentieth-century United States. The biggest change occurred in the 1930s with the advent of the adventure strip, produced by a new breed of comics artists who worked in a set of highly refined illustrational styles. Alex Raymond's *Flash Gordon*, Hal Foster's *Tarzan* and *Prince Valiant*, and Milton Caniff's *Terry and the Pirates* all featured beautiful and innovative draftsmanship devoted to chronicling the derring-do of fearless, right-thinking, physically perfect specimens of (white) manhood. Disreputable characters did not by any means entirely disappear from the comics pages, but they were definitely pushed off center stage by the new supermen (Clark Kent and Superman himself would emerge in the pages of the brand-new form of the comic book just before the end of the decade). Darger was still saving some of his favorite "bum" characters from the early strips as late as the 1960s. Leafing through his scrapbooks, one may still come across some of them alongside a full-page Sunday color comic of *Prince Valiant*. It was not as though Darger, the innovative designer of dozens of his own panoramic images, would have been insusceptible to the (comparably) remarkable beauty of Foster's pages. But, on the evidence of Darger's writing, one might say that Foster's pop-culture paragon of chivalry did not set him thinking and feeling with anything like the intensity that Fisher's Mutt and Jeff did.

During the same decade that the bums and rogues who dominated the early comic strips were seeing their primacy challenged by raven-locked knights in armor and young blond musclemen in space ships, another remarkable printing-and-publishing phenomenon of the early twentieth century was reaching the peak of its popularity. This was the pulp magazine, which wedded striking and often lurid visuals with hypersensational narratives of thrilling (and often extremely creepy) adventures. H. P. Lovecraft, Robert M. Howard, and their colleagues brought tales of weird horror and epic (as well as mock-epic) sword-and-sorcery to increasingly large audiences throughout the 1920s and 1930s. It is to the relations of their respective brands of "pulp history" (to use Carlo Rotella's phrase) to Darger's *Realms* that I shall now turn.[14]

Chapter 4

WEIRD FLESH, WORLD'S FLESH

DARGER AND THE PULPS

> The most merciful thing in the world, I
> think, is the inability of the human mind to
> correlate all its contents.
> —H. P. Lovecraft, "The Call of Cthulhu"

Of all the mass-mediated forms that Darger drew on for his work, perhaps none sets up as strong a field of resonances with it as the weird-tales school of pulp fiction that flourished in the 1920s and 1930s. Along with the narratives and images of virgin martyrs, victims and perpetrators of military carnage, and comic-strip bums and rogues that we have already considered, the highly atmospheric images of decay, perversion, abjection, defeat, and defiance that pervade the "weird horror" pulp of H. P. Lovecraft and his colleagues can help us understand some of the more disturbing features of *In the Realms*. One of the things that leafing through many of the old pulps—to be reminded of both their garish, lurid, and often kinky cover illustrations and their weird (and, again, often kinky) stories—makes abundantly clear is that the fascination with sometimes lethal and grotesque violence against young women and girls that has often been attributed in Darger to a private and personal pathology was actually a constitutive and quite public element of much of the mass or lowbrow fiction aimed at a presumptively male (and mostly young) readership in the decades between the world wars.

It is common knowledge that "pulp" magazines got their name from the very low-quality grade of newsprint on which they were printed. While acknowledging that, I want at the same time to invoke another sense of the word "pulp," which is "flesh." Pulp magazines are a densely fleshy medium, not least in the rapidity with which most of them have decayed into dust, but also in the spectacle of flesh—mostly, but not exclusively, female—that they often put on display on the cover. Flesh (mostly male in this case) has a tendency in pulp to get beaten to exactly that, while the weird-horror stories are designed to make the reader's flesh creep. In Lovecraft's weird-horror stories, nerdy young men from New England get overwhelmed by what Lovecraft called "the Ancient Ones," monsters of exorbitantly fishy fleshiness. In Robert E. Howard's "Conan" stories, erotic tableaus of the delectable flesh of muscular young bodies, male and female, alternate with scenes of carnage in which other bodies—often nonwhite—fall by the score beneath the hero's weapon.

Darger takes the "flesh-and-blood" fascinations of pulp to one of its extremes (but, as we shall see, other such extremes were in massively wide circulation in the period, from every newsstand and drugstore magazine rack), in his concern in some of his writings and paintings with the removal of internal organs from the mutilated bodies of some of the little girl victims of Glandelinian cruelty and violence in In the Realms. But rather than seeing this—or seeing it only—in the context of late-twentieth-century accounts of serial killers who keep their victims' livers in the fridge, I want to consider how Darger, like some of the best and most influential of his pulp-writing contemporaries, may have been experimenting in devising such bloody and hyperfleshy scenes with exploring generally taboo ways of thinking and feeling about the forms and modes of embodiment available to (or compulsory for) men and women, girls and boys, humans and animals, bosses and laborers, warriors and civilians in their world.

In some working notes for what turned out to be his unfinished book, The Visible and the Invisible, Maurice Merleau-Ponty speaks of "the Flesh of the body" as existing in a chiastic, interbraided way with "the Flesh of the world." He famously writes, in a note dated May 1960: "My body is made of the same flesh as the world . . . and . . . this flesh of my body is shared by the world, the world reflects it, encroaches upon it and it encroaches upon the world."[1] Not for him the supposedly simple and straightforward divisions between mind and body, self and world, that have subtended so much modern thought and alleged common sense. For Merleau-Ponty, the "flesh" is not only what we are used to thinking of, as a butcher might, as the potentially separable or detachable "meat" of a body, the material that lies beneath the skin and on the bone. The world is "flesh," too, and the flesh of bodies and the flesh of the world overlap. "Flesh" and "pulp" are in some ways also inextricable in his thinking about this. He writes further, in a note dated November 1960, of what he sees as the mutually "enclosing-enclosed" state of the relation of the body's flesh to the world's flesh: "The very pulp of the sensible, what is indefinable about in it, is nothing else than the union in it of the 'inside' with the 'outside,' the contact in thickness of self with self."[2] Rather than thinking of Darger and his fellow "weird" pulp writers as "pure sadists" (or "pure masochists"), "pure" would-be executioners, or "pure" would-be victims, I want to consider what difference it might make to try to imagine a context for their work in which bodies and world (or worlds) can be seen as in some senses sharing the nature and texture of flesh. The often rank misogyny that pervaded early twentieth-century US public and private life is a factor in much work by men (and some by women) that can be studied without either being accepted on its own terms ("that's just the way things were") or explained away on ours ("things are nothing like that now"). What else, in addition to manifesting some of the misogyny endemic to their (and, mutatis mutandis, our) world, were pulp writers in the 1920s and 1930s and after (including Darger, for argument's sake) up to, with their spectacular verbal and visual performances and demonstrations of the extreme durability and equally extreme vulnerability, beauty, hideousness, and general ubiquity of flesh? What do early twentieth-century writers and artists producing weird-horror pulp have to tell us about the doubly weird flesh of Darger's work, the frequently (in his term) "nuded" little girls with male genitals with which his paintings are crowded, and the mutilated and disemboweled child bodies that also sometimes figure in the work? These are the kinds of questions I want to try to palpate in the ensuing pages.

Darger and Lovecraft, Pulp Writers

No one would mistake Henry Darger and his girl warriors and girl martyrs for the denizens of H. P. Lovecraft's latter-day New England gothic. And yet, in some crucial ways, *In the Realms of the Unreal* shares some of the most indicative features of its moral cosmology with that of Lovecraft's realms. Darger's world, like Lovecraft's, occupies a cosmos that looks a lot like an everyday modern one in many ways—except that an irresistible, all-pervading demonic force tends to manifest itself at the dramatic climaxes of both writers' narratives with a terrible kind of regularity and punctuality. In a few classic tales of his such as "The Call of Cthulhu," "The Haunter of the Dark," and "The Shadow Out of Time," Lovecraft launched what came to be called the Cthulhu Mythos: a cosmological setting for stories whose main outlines suggest that humanity lives in a relatively small and fragile bubble, and that the long-term reality of life in the universe is a consequence of the existence of the Ancient Ones, the entities with names like Cthulhu, Nyarlathotep, and Yog-Sothoth, vast and mysterious entities who lie sleeping at the edge of the universe but who rouse themselves occasionally and devastate the order of things. Stories set in the Cthulhu Mythos often feature men or boys who get a glimpse of the power of the Ancient Ones and a complementary sense of the utter impotence and meaninglessness of human striving, and never recover from, or don't survive, the perception. The sheer immensity of being of the Ancient Ones so far outruns the human capacity to apprehend it that just the discrepancy of scale can fracture or destroy the mind that tries to apprehend it. Darger's Glandelinians, nasty lot though they are, pale in comparison with the immensity of evil that Lovecraft's Old Ones mete out to humanity with sublime indifference. Only in his vast and prolonged meteorological disasters does Darger go in for comparably intense ill effects.

This would all sound quite grim had the grandly named Cthulhu Mythos not been permeated from its inception, and to its ancient and rotten core, with hefty dollops of irony and self-parody. Lovecraft and several of his numerous correspondents among his fellow weird-fantasy pulp writers, Robert Howard included, delighted in recirculating and adding to the store of strange "Cthulhu" names and terrors—so much so that naive fans ever since have been trying to locate the *Necronomicon*, the made-up "occult" treatise in the pages of which Lovecraft's stories and their imitators suggested that one could get the lowdown on this stuff. The FAQ sections for the various Cthulhu Mythos websites routinely inform fledgling fans that the occult literature on Cthulhu doesn't really exist—and that also, by the way, this "dark" pop metaphysic has always been something of a shared gag among insiders. The really intense pleasure that the mythos and its fictions afford fans is that of oscillating between experiencing the chill of its bleakly nihilistic take on the place of the human in an empty cosmos and at the same time finding irresistible the invitation to treat this communal perception as a shared—indeed, a particular favorite—in joke.[3]

For all the considerable differences of manner and method between Lovecraft and Darger, one does find a somewhat similar kind of eerie fusion or confusion of immense cosmic threat with something like an inside joke in Darger's *In the Realms of the Unreal*. Darger specifies at certain points of *In the*

Realms that the Christian theology of salvation applies only to Earth; what Puritan preachers called the Gracious Merits of Christ's death on the Cross do not, for Darger, extend to the large planet of which Earth is a moon and, on which *In the Realms of the Unreal* takes place. Of course, Darger's occasional—but, I take it, significant—comments about the Christian scheme of salvation's not extending beyond Earth is massively contradicted almost everywhere else in *In the Realms* by the centrality to his story of the very existence of the pious Catholic nation of Abbieannia, its Catholic emperor, and his seven daughters, the Vivian Girls. Somewhat like trying to maintain the girl-boy distinction in a world where all girls appear to have penises and testicles, trying to understand how Catholicism and Christianity can be so enormously meaningful on a planet on which the Christian scheme of salvation has no purchase involves us in something at least highly paradoxical and potentially highly ironical.

Darger appears not to subscribe to the hallowed principle of noncontradiction; rather, I imagine him concurring with Walt Whitman: "Do I contradict myself? Very well then, I contradict myself."[4] One of Lovecraft's narrators expresses something like gratitude for what I take to be a similarly "nonchalant" (a favorite word of Whitman's) attitude when he writes, in the famous opening line of his story "The Call of Cthulhu," "The most merciful thing in the world, I think, is the inability of the human mind to correlate all its contents."[5] The pulps, Lovecraft's stories certainly included, are generally so full of "Ming the Merciless" and other embodiments and enactments of the inexorably and inhumanly cruel that when a pulp writer of Lovecraft's gifts has a narrator begin a story by pronouncing on what "the most merciful thing in the world" is, I for one want to sit up and listen: "the inability of the human mind to correlate all its contents."

It may be germane in considering this idea to note that Lovecraft in a sense led two lives. By his own account, until he was twenty-four, he lived in what sounds like almost unbroken solitude, "protected" from the outside world by his mother and other older relatives, but left largely alone by them. In 1914, at the age of twenty-four, he was invited to join a large national amateur writers' association that helped members circulate their work and hosted annual conventions (those who think that "zines" came into existence in the seventies are right—only it was the 1870s and not the 1970s that saw the first explosion of self-published periodicals authored and distributed to each other by groups of amateur writers). Lovecraft, who had in some ways lived into early adulthood almost without benefit of society, quickly rose through the organization's ranks to serve as its national president. This amateur writers' association, Lovecraft once wrote, gave him what his immediate familial circumstances had failed to deliver: "life itself."[6] Through it, he developed the extensive and enduring network of fellow writers with whom he corresponded, and he met Sonia Greene, a former president of the national association and the Jewish woman whom he astonished his elderly WASP relatives by marrying and moving to New York City to live with. The marriage failed within a couple of years, and Lovecraft moved back home to Providence, Rhode Island, where he then wrote several of his most influential stories, including the "Cthulhu" ones. Despite his spectacular-looking conversion from extreme loner to ceaseless networker (largely by mail), Lovecraft's highly socialized adult self was obviously haunted by his weird, antisocial other self. In the course of the 1930s, toward the end of his life, he largely reverted to his solitary ways, living on almost no money, often eating what sounds like disgusting food, and dying in his mid-forties of intestinal cancer that he declined to have treated medically until it was far too late (while also maintaining to the very end of his life a remarkably extensive and spirited correspondence with his fellow pulp writers).

I think of Darger's most active years—illustrating his work and continuing it beyond the first twenty or thirty years of his adult life, when he seems to have written most of In the Realms and to have become intensely involved in beginning to illustrate his work—as being roughly analogous to the hypersocial middle period of Lovecraft's life. Darger never really abandoned the solitary ways in which Lovecraft grew up and to which he eventually returned, for the most part. But to my mind, Darger also lived two lives, the isolated one that his neighbors and co-workers could observe and the other one that was what we might call a riot of association through appropriation, however quiet a riot it may have been. About halfway through, Darger appears to have given up on, or at least put aside and never got back to, his project of arranging and binding the fifteen thousand pages of In the Realms into sequenced volumes. Perhaps in the midst of this monumental task he opted for—as Lovecraft's narrator had—the self-administered "mercy" of ultimately not collating the contents of his mind, as these contents had manifested themselves in his saga. It should not surprise us, then, that In the Realms of the Unreal has two logically incompatible endings. In one, the "good guys," the pious Christian forces—Emperor Vivian, his generals, the Vivian sisters, and their surviving child allies—win the war and subdue the cruel and heathen Glandelinian armies. In the other, the last we see of the Glandelinian soldiers is when they anticlimactically ride away from the signing of the peace treaty laughing and singing in chorus (in Jessica Yu's documentary, to the tune of "The Battle Hymn of the Republic" or "John Brown's Body"), "We were only, only fooling, / We were only, only fooling."[7] And so, in that alternate ending, the war wears on, perhaps into eternity, beyond even Darger's perseverance.

Darger, Howard, and "Pulp History"

At first glance, Robert Howard might seem even less likely than Lovecraft to provide a basis of comparison with Darger. But as with Lovecraft, an ongoing existential and ethical crisis at the heart of his work imbues Howard's writing with a kind of tension that it shares with the work of the other two writers. In the case of each, I believe, there is an irresolvable and, to use Lovecraft's terms, uncorrelatable tension in their work between one part of the fantasy and another, and between one part of the author's experience and another, which is probably what makes the "pulp" they produced so compelling to so many readers, down to the present day. The second thing most readers learn about Robert Howard—after the fact that he wrote the Conan stories—is that he committed suicide by shooting himself in the head at the age of thirty, in 1936, after hearing that his mother, who had been ill for many years, was finally dying. In most ways, the matter of Howard's stories contrasts strongly with Lovecraft's or Darger's. Howard's stories tend to be about freebooting men's men who try to reach far into themselves and far into history or prehistory to maintain some kind of integrity, some kind of peace with their code of honor, in a world of extreme and inescapable violence. Howard's stories are loved by their fans for their somewhat melancholy and self-reflective way of relating larger historical lost causes to their heroes'—Conan's and others'—involvement in an endless cycle of bloody conflict interrupted by idyllic periods of peace and sexual and romantic union, which are themselves interrupted, in turn, by more bloody conflict. Scenes of combat and battle come and go in Howard's stories, as they do in Darger's, but war can never end more than conditionally, as it does in the two alternative endings Darger composed for *In the Realms*, with the "happy ending"—"the War is Over"—sitting uncomfortably and unaccommodatedly side by side with the ending in which the treaty signers march away, laughing and singing, "we were only fooling."

Howard and his Conan stories, along with his other pulp hero cycles, are only now, seventy years after his death, receiving the scholarly attention of careful editing and reprinting and extensive critical consideration. Howard's defenders, some of whom are currently deeply engaged in trying to get him recognized as an author and even as a canonical author, feel obliged to combat the interpretation that L. Sprague Decamp, one of Howard's biographers in the 1970s at the height of the *Conan* movie-cycle phase, put into circulation when he argued (along well-rutted Freudian tracks) that Howard's suicide was a consequence of overwhelming oedipal tensions that he felt toward his parents.[8] Students of Howard's work who have read through his extensive opus—poetry as well as prose; long, revealing letters (to Lovecraft among others) as well as stories—say that Howard had been debating the question of suicide with himself, his correspondents, and his readers even before his mother became seriously ill.

Like Howard's suicide around the time of his mother's death, Darger's attachment to little girls has also mostly been read in the context of a fairly conservative Freudian oedipal scenario: Darger's mother died when he was not quite four years old, after giving birth to a little girl who was immediately given up for adoption and apparently passed completely out of Darger's life along with his mother. Darger's most influential Freudian interpreter, John MacGregor, interprets Darger's fascination with girls and much of the violence his narratives wreak on them as signs of Darger's difficulty or failure in coming to terms with his feelings of grief and mourning over having lost his mother and his newborn sister when he was so young—as well as with the very different, in some ways inassimilable, feeling of anger at his sister that it was her birth that had deprived him of his mother. "Weird" pulps of the kind that Lovecraft and Howard (and, as I am arguing in this chapter, in a sense Darger) produced were especially fertile and productive sites for exploring and experiencing such contradictory realities, social and political as well as familial. I propose also to argue that an intense and hyperviolent misogyny was, generally speaking, "weird" pulp's most frequent recourse for grounding or ungrounding its depictions and evocations of these highly contradictory states of perception. In doing so, I want to explore some of the ways in which the frequent recursion in Darger's work to violence against girls may well be less a personal pathology of his (as accounts such as MacGregor's tend to suggest) and more something that he shared to a great extent with many of his male pulp-writing (and, in much greater numbers, male pulp-reading) contemporaries.

Anyone trying to understand the wide and powerful appeal of pulp fiction among proletarian readers of the 1920s and 1930s would do well to recognize how powerfully and often violently emotional much pulp fiction is.[9] There is a very pronounced tendency in literary and cultural studies of the early twenty-first century to deprecate and sidestep the violently emotional, as part of a received notion of what it means to be "against" violence, or "against" the many kinds of impulses and acts that get lumped together into the catchall category of violence. The mythology pervasive in our time and place is that violence is always the consequence of some trauma suffered by the perpetrator of the violence. If violence had not previously been done to this perpetrator of violence, this line of thinking goes, he or she would never have acted violently.

But for all the concepts and assumptions that I would like to see jettisoned from the standard oedipalizing Freudian repertoire, one insight of Freud's that I want to hold on to, almost as a talisman, is his perception that anger, rage, and aggression are not only secondary effects in human affect and behavior, damages imposed from the outside on an ostensibly innocent subject as trauma. Feelings of anger, rage, and aggression are familiar to most of us, traumatized and untraumatized alike, quite possibly from the earliest months of our lives. What I believe the often violent, and violently emotional, pages of pulp fiction afford us is a kind of vast elaborative literature in which we can imagine at least to some degree owning some of our own violently emotional impulses rather than altogether disavowing and denying them. Perhaps more than any other of Freud's revisers, Melanie Klein has had the most to teach us about the range of intense negative affects, whose feeling and expression are, according to her, a major part of the task of being a normal infant and toddler. Or so we may gather from Klein's remarkable theory of the furious infant that hallucinates invading its mother's body, wreaking havoc on it and (here Klein is at her most proleptically Dargeresque) triumphantly and cleverly stealing from it the multiple phalluses of the father that the infant (again, according to Klein) hallucinates that the mother stores in the wonderland of her richly endowed and sometimes frustratingly withheld "insides."[10]

On the rare occasions when Darger characterizes his own relation to his writing and the kinds of stories it tells, he speaks of himself as a historian. We may take him at his word as some kind of historian, but a historian with a difference—a historian of the unreal, or perhaps the half-real. I want to experiment with taking the kinds of "wild" theoretical fictions that Klein risked telling about the psychic and emotional lives of infants along with the kinds of "wild" and weird cosmic thrillers that Lovecraft and Howard—and, I am arguing, Darger—tell in the context of "Pulp History," the innovative idea of the American studies scholar Carlo Rotella. He writes: "Pulp History is to the history taught and written in the academy as pulp fiction is to canonical literature: wilder, more eventful, less encumbered by the demands of verisimilitude, darkly suspicious of standard-issue cultural credentials as signs of intellectual timidity or even of complicity in some elite plot against regular folks. Pulp history rips away the veil—the official version according to accredited experts—to reveal alternative accounts of human affairs ranging from almost outright fantasy to arguments that earnestly question the received historical record."[11] Rotella's article is primarily interested in a special strain of Harvard professor who (in generation after generation, as he tells it) tosses his or her ultra-respectable credentials aside to take up an unpopular—indeed, professionally indefensible—hobbyhorse such as the lost continent of Atlantis or alien abduction. Rotella's chief specimen is Eben Norton Horsford, a nineteenth-century Brahmin who became obsessed with his "discovery" (on the basis of evidence ranging from sparse to nonexistent) that Leif Ericson and his ax-wielding fellow Vikings had colonized the Boston area a millennium before.

I want to bring to the foreground a part of Rotella's argument that he treats as secondary: the use of "pulp history" (perhaps especially as practiced by popular pulp writers) as a kind of alternative history that keeps alive, in however distorted form, some aspect of a past that seems to be left out of or actively suppressed in the received or quasi-official historical record. Here, the discussion in chapter 2 of the traces of histories of massacre in the "adult juvenilia" (or pulp fiction) of both Darger and Branwell Brontë is pertinent: both men's accounts of war are haunted by an excess of horror in response to the vast amounts of pain and suffering inflicted on and by soldiers, and inflicted on civilian populations, especially the more vulnerable among them—women, children, the old, the poor, and the infirm. "Pulp history" undertakes the complex and quite possibly impossible task of preserving some record (however imperfect) of actual sufferings at the same time it aspires to provide some comfort, however belated and ultimately ineffectual, to sufferers (and to readers who may suffer "for" the violated, or imagine themselves doing or wanting to do so). In this connection, Rotella's own account of his adolescent reading experience of Robert Howard's Conan stories as both stirring and "soothing" is illuminating. Rotella provides an extensive discussion of how he was first moved to feel a passion for the interdisciplinary study of history and its cognate fields by his voracious appetite as a teenager for what he now sees as the exemplary pulp history of the Conan stories. Rotella says that in his early youth he would read a Conan book fifteen or twenty times, magnetized by its sweeping sense of (an alternative) history, but also "soothed" by Howard's "forward-pressing style, well-suited to its subject, tend[ing] to runs of rolling prose punctuated with adverbial clunks and awkward flashes of forced poetic effect, like a bebop soloist backed by a drummer dropping bombs off the beat."[12] He adduces the following passage from "Red Nails"—about Conan's coming to the rescue of "a she-pirate named Valeria" from an attacker—as both illustrative and characteristic of Howard's prose and of his "soothing" (for all its outward kineticism) version of pulp history:

> She reached down with her left hand and gripped [her attacker's] long hair, forcing his head back so that the white teeth and rolling eyes gleamed up at her. The tall Xotalanc cried out fiercely and leaped in, smiting with all the fury of his arm. Awkwardly she parried the stroke, and it beat the flat of her blade down on her head so that she saw sparks flash before her eyes, and staggered. Up went the sword again, with a low, beast-like cry of triumph—and then a giant form [Conan] loomed behind the Xotalanc and steel flashed like a jet of blue lightning. The cry of the warrior broke short and he went down like an ox beneath the pole-ax, his brains gushing from his skull that had been split to the throat.[13]

Substitute a lamb for an ox, and a Vivian Girl for the buxom she-pirate, and we are not far from the endless-seeming bloody pulp (as in "beaten to a pulp") history of Darger's In the Realms of the Unreal. Rotella's account of his experience may help us understand how Darger (and, potentially, the reader or viewer of his work) may find rich sources of both stimulation and excitement on the one hand, and some considerable degree of comfort and consolation on the other hand, in his narratives and paintings.

In his article, Rotella resolves his relation to Howard's writing by distancing himself from it as an adult, seeing it then as a search for a "usable past" on young Howard's part, in which a heroic breed of "barbarians" ("nativist" white frontiersmen) struggle valiantly and even successfully to turn back the tide of encroaching modernization, immigration, and urbanization in the United States.[14] Darger's work is no doubt susceptible to some of the same kinds of political and historical critique: that it embodies a vast fantasy about a war to end slavery, "based"—insofar as it is based on any real referent—on the Civil War, only a version of it in which all the slaves appear to be white children. But I want to claim more for *In the Realms* as "pulp history" than seeing it only as one of the things it may indeed be, the product of yet another scheme (witting or not) for the continuation of white supremacy in the United States by other means. As the work of someone who had been institutionalized for years early in his life for alleged feeblemindedness, a life circumstance that seems to have been determinate in setting the tone for the far-under-the-radar way of living that Darger cultivated his entire adult life, Darger's writing and drawing provides a rare (although by no means unique) archive of extensive cultural production by a twentieth-century American urban subaltern. One of the ways of specifying the nature of this particular set of cultural productions is not only to notice the work's silent disavowal of the raced history of slavery in the United States, but also to relate it to the history of the "bound" boys and girls who were indentured and held in a virtual state of slavery. Indentured servitude (as it was called) was the fate of many orphans; it could have been Darger's—indeed, some would say that his sixty years' employment at the minimum wage as a menial worker was itself a form of indenture, except that, remarkably, he still managed to eke both ample time and materials (such as they were) out of the severely limited economic means at his disposal. Having been forced to spend his entire life in such a state of servitude, it's no wonder that Darger found his most reliable subject in imagining the doings and experiences of a vast class of child slaves in rebellion against their cruel masters.

Catholic Popular Representation and (Female) Bodies in Extremis

I want in this section to consider the relation of Darger's subaltern status and the kind of alternative or pulp history he chronicled not only to the religious culture in which he actively participated (both as a frequent communicant at his neighborhood parish church, and as a secret maker of religious art and narrative) but also to various other religious cultures in the early-twentieth-century United States as they were being recast in a range of forms of mass culture, from high- to lowbrow. The manifestations of recognizably Jewish, Protestant, and Roman Catholic motifs in pulp magazines and their most notable successor form at the newsstand, superhero comic books, are of particular help in recognizing the pulp elements in Darger's work.

The ostensibly specifically Jewish elements of psychoanalysis as it was formulated by Freud and reformulated by him and his circle have been the object of much scholarly consideration in recent years.[15] Melanie Klein's work is no doubt part of this story, but so (as recent historians of mass culture have made clear) is the emergence of the superhero form of visual and verbal narration in the work of two young Jewish men barely out of their teens on the eve of the Second World War.[16] Rarely juxtaposed with superhero comics, Klein's theories about infantile fantasy and the fantasized magical powers of the phallus and the maternal breast or body are in some ways highly compatible with the fantasies of invulnerability and superpotency that impel *The Adventures of Superman*. The television show based on the *Superman* comics premiered in 1952 and ran until 1958. During those years, I was one of the countless little boys who thrilled to the spectacle of Superman flying on television (to the accompaniment of martial music), and I'm sure I was not the only one who then excitedly ran around the house until dinnertime dressed in underwear and a towel "Superman cape." I was eight when the media reported that the *Superman* star George Reeves had killed himself, and it was one of my first difficult lessons in trying to distinguish beloved characters and fantasy objects from real people.

But Superman and his ilk of course did not emerge full grown; they developed gradually out of the pulp heroes of the previous generation or two like Nick Carter, Tarzan, Conan, and Flash Gordon. Many of these heroes, in their close resemblance to the ranking heroes of Anglo-American colonialism and imperialism (from Allen Quatermain to Indiana Jones), look thoroughly Protestant, given the extremely high degree of rugged-male individualism and self-reliance they are supposed to embody. But also apparent in the proliferation of superheroes, including its spread across gender (a mere two years separates the first appearance of *Superman* from that of *Wonder Woman*), is a strain of fantasy that is also highly compatible with some strains of early twentieth-century popular Catholic piety. Popular devotion to the Virgin Mary in her roles as divine mother and mediator (protector of women and children, guardian of anguished femininity and humanity, and so on) is crucial to the vernacular theology that informs Darger's work and the world he inhabited. This fantasy world is in some obvious ways highly compatible with both the world of pulp fiction and Klein's accounts of infantile fantasies, in which mothers and their bodies oscillate with dizzying instability between positions of thorough abjection and those of unbreechable superpotency.

Catholics had been producing and consuming writing and images that were either pulp or proto-pulp for a long time before Frank Munsey's *Argosy* (commonly considered to have been the first pulp magazine) began publication in 1896. For much Catholic theology, both official and popular, incarnation is a centrally compelling and highly charged mystery, one that ranks alongside or even exceeds in interest the more general Christian concerns with revelation and salvation. Many pulp stories and cover illustrations, like many Catholic narratives and images, are situated peculiarly, even uncannily, close to skin, bone, and flesh, the most readily palpable (a word with the same root as "pulp") parts of the human body—and often close to the skin, bone, and flesh of bodies in circumstances of extreme duress. The human body in extremis is often the focus of readerly fascination in the pulps, as it is the focus of pity and awe (and, consciously or not, erotic desire) in much pious religious devotion.

The Blessed Anne Emmerich, as she is known to Catholics, was an early nineteenth-century German nun and writer who dictated elaborate, and often extremely violent, visions that she had of Jesus's sufferings; her accounts have never been out of print in the past two hundred years. In fact, several editions of them in English translation have been continuously available at Borders and Barnes and Noble since Mel Gibson drew heavily on her writings for his 2004 film gore fest, The Passion of the Christ. Although rendered doubly strange and uncanny by being largely relocated in a child population, Darger's fascination with the body, with flesh and bone at its most densely material and often in great duress, seems to me to fall well within the larger tradition of this kind of proto-pulp of which early twentieth-century weird-fantasy pulp seems a not-very-distant descendant. Like Mel Gibson, Darger also channels Anne Emmerich's gruesome and gory writing, reproducing it in In the Realms (at least at one point) at length and verbatim, and to remarkable effect. To the canonical gospel scene of Jesus's being scourged and to Emmerich's gruesome and elaborate reimagining of the violent scene, Darger adds the remarkable "detail" that the nude Jesus becomes sexually aroused as he is scourged and that the terrible pain he is already enduring is compounded by the shame he feels as his tormentors turn his body so that his erect penis is exposed to his mother's gaze. This is (in its highly conflicted way) one of the only explicit depictions of sexual self-consciousness and extreme embarrassment (interlined with an infantile wish to expose one's erect penis to one's mother) that any of Darger's readers have reported discovering in his work. But part of the effect of Emmerich's own sensationalization (which appears to have shown Mel Gibson the way) of Jesus's extreme physical sufferings has been to render all but explicit the high level of eroticism latent in the canonical depictions of Jesus stripped, beaten, and crucified before a crowd of callous torturers and tormented followers. In a sense, Darger has only connected the dots that, in such pious and hyperviolent retellings of the Passion story as Emmerich's, link the tortured body of Jesus to quite other kinds of scenes of physical exposure, intimacy, and vulnerability.

Some of the tension between embracing and at least outwardly disavowing such pleasures—central ones in much pulp fiction—was manifest in the distance between the cover illustration and the narrative content of the classic pulp magazine *Weird Tales*. In their letters to each other, H. P. Lovecraft and Robert Howard—both leading contributors to the magazine—express a shared embarrassment about the lurid and kinky style of covers that appeared on its issues. Many of these were drawn by Margaret Brundage, a Chicago artist whose many color cover illustrations for *Weird Tales* characteristically featured one nude or scantily clothed young woman being bound and spanked or whipped by another, or menaced with a knife, often in a harem setting—a recognizable form of girl-on-girl sadomasochism aimed primarily at straight male readers.[17] Lovecraft declined to work "spicy" interludes into his stories to match these covers. Howard also generally ignored them, but he did include some "action" between young women in at least a few of his stories, including some of the most highly regarded ones, such as the aforementioned "Red Nails" (1936). However, he denies catering to the taste for prurience in a letter to Lovecraft in which he comments that readers looking for stories to match the kinky covers of *Weird Tales* can find them among the contributions of his and Lovecraft's colleague and correspondent Seabury Quinn, whose long series of stories featuring "occult detective" Jules de Grandin made his work even more popular by a substantial margin than that of Lovecraft or Howard.

Quinn may indeed have owed some of his popularity with the early, largely male, pulp readership to his penchant for giving narrative space to the kinds of sexy bits featured on the covers. Many modern readers may feel repelled but unsurprised by Lovecraft's misogyny of omission—that is, his strong tendency simply to leave women and girls out of his stories—which is a common flaw in both pulp and respectable twentieth-century fiction aimed at men. For all his popularity in the heyday of pulp, Quinn is relatively very little read today beyond a tiny circle of pulp cultists. Part of the reason for this may be that Jules de Grandin's "occult detections" have come to look irredeemably hokey over the years, but it may also be that the extreme misogyny of some of Quinn's work has also made it increasingly unappealing. The degree of violence against women depicted in some of his work far exceeds the mild, fairly balletic kink of Brundage's cover drawings. His only novel-length Jules de Grandin tale, *The Devil's Bride* (serialized in *Weird Tales* in 1932), features scenes of spectacularly atrocious violence against women: one is crucified, and another is blinded after having had her hands cut off and her tongue cut out. Far from being anomalous or singular in this regard, Quinn is apparently imitating similar material from what had been an international bestseller not long before, a novel titled *The Sorcerer's Apprentice* by the internationally acclaimed author Hanns Heinz Ewers (published in German in 1910 and in an English translation in 1927), in which a young man is forced not only to see his bride crucified but also to pierce her side with a pitchfork as she hangs dying. When Quinn writes about young women tortured by unfeeling soldiers or a baby sacrificed at a Black Mass on the back of a kneeling female nude, the mise-en-scène resembles to a notable degree those recurrent scenes in Darger in which girl warriors are captured, stripped of their clothing, beaten, maimed, and executed by Glandelinian soldiers. These scenes in Darger's work may still disturb us, but they look less anomalous, and considerably less like evidence of extreme personal pathology, when we discover that similar scenes were not at all uncommon in a wide range of male-authored fiction of the 1920s and 1930s.

Tales and images of women being crucified are of course not only a product of twentieth-century popular writing. They extend forward from medieval accounts of now-obscure women saints who were martyred on the cross to the kind of overheated "decadent" drawings and paintings of a century and more ago that prepared the way for the ostensibly artistically ambitious writing of Hanns Heinz Ewers (the English translation of his *Sorcerer's Apprentice* had been made by Ludwig Lewisohn, a prominent anti-assimilationist US Jewish intellectual in the mid-twentieth century) as well as the sensationally misogynistic pulp pages of Seabury Quinn. In a brief but informative survey of the figure of the crucified woman, the critic Rachel Anderson brings together numerous images ranging from sixteenth-century paintings of the martyrdom (by crucifixion) of Saint Julia of Corsica in Italian churches and palaces (including Hieronymus Bosch's in the Palazzo Ducale in Venice) to computer-generated images on pornographic websites.[18] A scene of a girl either (depending on one's point of view) masturbating with a crucifix or being raped with a crucifix by the devil is one of the scenes that shocked its way into the memory of millions of viewers of the film adaptation of

William Peter Blatty's 1971 novel *The Exorcist*. Despite the feelings of horror that the 1973 film's scenes of all-out demonic possession induce—or because of them—these scenes (especially that of the head of the child actress Linda Blair furiously turning completely around) have been among the most frequently parodied in modern cinema. As is the case with Lovecraft and his collaborators' "Cthulhu Mythos," a scene of violence and terror that may shock and frighten young or first-time viewers may eventually come to be regarded by significant numbers of repeat or older viewers as a kind of in-joke.

In our states of physical pain or sexual arousal, and in our uncanny moments of awareness (fitful as these may be) that our relation to gender may be much more labile and complex than most of us are used to thinking that it is, the flesh (our own) that most of us take so much for granted most of the time may in a thrilling or horrifying moment come to seem, creepily, to be someone else's, or weird flesh. Writers of weird-tales-style pulp in the 1920s and 1930s elaborated many ways of both minimizing and exaggerating the capacity for ordinary (our own) flesh becoming transformed (sometimes with a simple shift of mood or perspective) into weird, alien flesh. Would-be pious narrators of Roman Catholic virgin-martyr narratives strive to make their readers see the spectacle of mortified, tortured flesh as the condition of being to which all devout persons should aspire—while at the same time risking, wittingly or not, the possibility that their readers may also become turned on by the scene of extreme physical vulnerability and exposure that they are being invited to witness.

A posthumously published novel by Seabury Quinn, titled *Alien Flesh* (1977), which had apparently been written as a pulp serial considerably earlier (circa 1953), provides some clues about the intense, melodramatic, and often violent erotics of weird-fantasy pulp and the form's penchant for self-parody. *Alien Flesh* tells the story of a rising star among US Egyptologists named Lynne Foster (a graduate of Amherst College who had recently earned a Ph.D. in archaeology from Harvard) who, tearing through heavy traffic in Cairo, becomes partially responsible for the death of a girl of a good Muslim family who is about to be married. The girl's angry and grief-stricken father exacts a terrible revenge on young Foster: he hires *slubbia* (necromancers) to abduct Foster and to transform his body into that of his recently deceased daughter, Ismet. In this pulp fiction of Quinn's, it is interestingly the male body that is subjected to torture, the virtual crucifixion to which Quinn (and other writers such as Ewers) had elsewhere subjected female characters' bodies, as the Egyptian necromancers pierce, cut, and otherwise surgically transform the body of Lynne Foster, a strapping twenty-something all-American male, into that of a beautiful and barely nubile Muslim girl.

As Quinn tells the story, his athletic and virile protagonist has to become "inwardly" as well as physically female before he can experience genuine sexual desire or sexual pleasure again. The path of psychological and emotional gender transformation turns out to be a long one, as Quinn depicts it. It begins with the mature American man, who has precipitously been transferred into the Egyptian girl's body, discovering (to "Lynne's" astonishment and "Ismet's" delight) the surpassing intensities of sadomasochism from the receiver's side. When Ismet teases and annoys the elderly husband to whom she has been given, she discovers that although he may not be much in the vanilla-sex department, he's a dab hand with a rattan whip:

> The first few blows stung terribly, but before he'd given half a dozen cuts I discovered there was something stimulating—almost pleasant—in the pain, and something even more pleasing in the sensation of being dominated. It's hard to put into words and make it sound sensible, but somehow I found joy in knowing I was in his power, helpless and defenseless, and every blow he gave me added to the odd, elated feeling of complete submission. When he threw the cane aside I crept up to him, seized his hand and covered it with kisses.[19]

The next time she's alone with her husband, Ismet tries to tease him into whipping her again, but this time he hands her over to the guards to be swaddled in silk, tied up in an uncomfortable position, and left in a subterranean cell to contemplate her misdeeds at length.

After escaping from the harem and engaging in a further round of intrigues and adventures set in (where else?) Paris, Ismet decides to return to "his" home in the United States, where she seeks out and, very much against her nearly iron will, finds herself falling deeply in love with Lynne's former best buddy, the hunky Hugh Arundel. Through a series of excruciatingly difficult social encounters, the gorgeous and winsome young Ismet eventually "comes out" to Arundel as his former best friend Lynne Foster, come back to him in another body. Lynne, deeply disturbed at first by the loving and supportive Hugh's attempts to hold "his" hand or gaze fondly into "his" eyes, ultimately discovers in falling in love with Hugh a willingness to forget entirely about "his" past life as an entitled American guy, and to wax ecstatic about the prospect of bearing Hugh's babies. In the romantic sunset-with-rainbow ending the book tries to bring off, Ismet speaks of "slough[ing] off" her "Western patina" as "the *Muslima*—the real I—takes over."[20]

When Ismet finally entirely accepts herself as a young Muslim woman "destined" to marry the best male friend of "her" former male self, Lynne Foster, she tells Hugh that the process of coming to accept her profound feelings of love for him has "for months . . . been a rack on which my heart was torn to bleeding bits." She continues: "And all the time I've been in terror . . . that any moment you would penetrate my disguise and see Lynne Foster underneath the masquerade of woman's flesh" (231). Here, the book's logic of gender reaches a tipping point that reveals the fundamental dynamic driving the obsession of so much pulp writing by men with the exposure and piercing or penetration of women's or girl's bodies: the misogynistic fantasy that not only is femininity a masquerade, but that female flesh, female bodies, actually "weirdly" cover, conceal within themselves, trap, and imprison male beings and male desire. Male fantasies of crucifying, stabbing, and otherwise radically exposing and violently rending female bodies turn out to be about revealing and releasing the male pleasure and subjectivity fantasmatically lodged in those bodies. The story unsatisfyingly ends by suggesting that Lynne's real desire, erotic and otherwise, has not actually been transmuted into a woman's desire but that the desire of the woman into whom Lynne has been transformed almost automatically turns into Hugh's desire as soon as she accepts his love and desire for her. Ismet, who has set two continents on fire with her beauty, gets effectively "killed off" as a character (and as a desiring subject) as she prepares to march down the aisle with the best friend of the man who accidentally killed her at the beginning of the novel.

Besides this depressing and familiar dismissal, however, there may yet be another, more forbidden fantasy, concealed inside this one. The second fantasy takes the form of an envious and often resentful male suspicion that women and girls have access by virtue of their gender to kinds and intensities of sexual experience and pleasure about which men can only fantasize (or read about in weird-tales pulp fiction). Lying perhaps only partially occluded in some of Darger's most violent scenes of the beating and dismemberment of some of the girl warriors in his work may be a similar mixture of envy and admiration for a thoroughly girlish form of the New Woman of the period of his childhood and youth—from Mary Pickford to Shirley Temple. Darger appears to have found this new and novel style of femininity so appealing that ordinary attraction (personal and sexual) "boils over" into both intense (albeit partial) identification and (at the same time) extreme fear and perhaps loathing. Early in *In the Realms*, Darger writes that although some girls (and boys) may be weak and vulnerable, it is a widely known fact that the toughest girls are tougher than any boys. Who knows what early experiences of late fantasies of Darger's may subtend his confident assertion of this "fact"? Let us take the boy genitals with which he depicts so many of his "nuded" heroines as a sign that he declined to resolve the matter that vexes so many of his fellow pulp writers, the transformation of "weird flesh" (between genders and between "races," as in Lynne Foster's metamorphosis from WASP male to hyperfeminine Muslim girl) back into some normal state. Flesh in Darger tends to stay weird. Perhaps that is the most lasting sign of the legacy of pulp in his work—and of pulp's largely foreclosed promise of providing alternative histories of childhood and other conditions that Darger sees as forms of slavery, abuse, and atrocity.

From Superhero Worship to Psycho Culture

Henry Darger himself has been the object of some posthumous fear and loathing, insofar as his work has been associated in the minds of some of its readers and viewers with pedophilia, sadism, and even serial murder. The stereotype of the creepy old man who preys on children was already well-established in the mass media in Darger's early adulthood, culminating in the sensational trial of sixty-four-year-old Albert Fish, the so-called Vampire of Brooklyn, in March 1935. Fish claimed to have been molested and beaten as a child and to have then pursued a life of self-torture and of the abduction and torture of children as an adult. By the time he was brought to trial, Fish was extravagantly claiming to have murdered—and to have violated and devoured the corpses of—children all over the country. Despite testimony by expert witnesses for the defense that Fish was insane, he was found guilty by a jury, condemned to death by the presiding judge, and executed by electrocution at Sing Sing in January 1936.

One of the defense's witnesses was Fredric Wertham, known at the time as an expert on child development and forensic psychiatry. He testified that Fish was the most deranged human being he had ever encountered in his wide professional experience. Wertham achieved national fame twenty years later when his book-length attack on the comic book industry (*Seduction of the Innocent*, 1954) inspired a congressional investigation and the subsequent institution of a Comic Books Code to try to ensure the wholesomeness of the then enormously popular medium. Wertham has been ridiculed in recent years for insisting that superhero comics of the postwar period were exposing a generation of American children to fetishistic, sadomasochistic, and otherwise perverted sexualities, but doing just that is now known to have been not entirely outside the conscious intentions of the inventor and chronicler of one of the most popular superhero figures, Wonder Woman. William Moulton Marston was a Harvard-trained psychologist who had been involved in the development and popularization of "lie-detector" technology. He had given an interview in *Parents* magazine in the early 1940s in which he deplored (as Wertham would, a decade later) the alleged effects of the comic books of the day on child readers, which provoked the comics publisher Charles Gaines to invite Marston to consult on how comics could wield their considerable influence more responsibly and effectively. Marston lived in what appears to have been a highly stable *ménage à trois* with his wife, Elizabeth Holloway Marston, and a former student named Olive Byrne, with both of whom he is said to have had children (the two women lived on together for over thirty years after Marston's untimely death). He later claimed that it was his wife, herself a professional psychologist, who had insisted that he develop a female superhero, and that he had taken both her and Olive Byrne as models for the new Wonder Woman character.

Henry Darger's fascination with little girls as exemplars of courage in combat may seem at least marginally less weird when one considers the enormous popularity of the comic-book exploits of Marston's Amazon superhero for years after her introduction in 1941. For all the protofeminist significance Marston's invention was later seen as having had (Wonder Woman's image was featured on the cover of the first issue of *Ms.* magazine), the early years of the comic over which Marston presided have a clear focus of erotic appeal: female-female bondage. Marston's earlier research on the psychological meanings of sorority initiation rituals took on new life in his comic. On page after page, in adventure after adventure, the comic in its early years looks like an only slightly modified update of Margaret Brundage's girl-on-girl bondage-and-discipline covers for 1930s *Weird Tales*.

Finally, in September 1943, a devoted reader of the comic, a staff sergeant in the US Army, sent a heartfelt message to Gaines in the form of a letter:

> I am one of those odd, perhaps unfortunate men who derive an extreme
> erotic pleasure from the mere thought of a beautiful girl, chained or

bound, or masked, or wearing extreme high-heels or high-laced boots,—in fact, any sort of constriction or strain whatsoever. Your tales of *Wonder Woman* have fascinated me on account of this queer "twist" in my psychological make-up. . . . Have you the same interest in bonds and fetters that I have? Have you studied such implements of confinement as you picture and write about? Have you actual references to such items as the "Brank," the leather mask, or the wide iron collar from Tibet, or the Green ankle manacle? Or do you just "dream" up these things?[21]

Gaines forwarded the letter to Marston with his own worried-sounding addition: "This is one of the things I've been afraid of, without quite being able to put my finger on it." He proposed such corrective measures as reducing "the use of chains" in the stories "by at least 50 to 75%," and Marston agreed.

But Marston's apparent fondness for images of young women subjecting each other to physical restraint—widely shared as this may have been among his readership—may not have been the actual focus of either his primary public or personal investment in *Wonder Woman*. Far from holding (as many of his male readers may have done) that men are essentially dominating creatures and women naturally submissive, Marston publicly believed something that was more like the reverse. He maintained in interviews, articles, and personal correspondence that everyone, men and women alike, longed to be bound by the kinds of "love chains" that he believed women had a special gift for forging and wielding—and not just on each other. And men longed to be captivated and in this sense lastingly captured by women. "The only hope for peace," Marston had written to his publisher six months before the sergeant's letter, "is to teach people who are full of pep and unbound force to *enjoy* being bound—*enjoy* submission to kind authority." In the following year he wrote that, when he had come to comics, he had considered their "worst offense" to be what he called "their blood-curdling masculinity"—hence his invention of a superwoman to enact his thoroughly gendered gospel of "restraint." Marston projected his vision far into the future, giving it messianic and utopian significance, opining to the *New York Times* in 1937 that "within 100 years the country will see the beginning of a sort of Amazonian matriarchy" that, through centuries of conflict, would in the course of the coming millennium establish itself as the unchallenged form of political and social life in the United States.[22]

Once again, Darger's highly elaborated fantasy of the supereminence of the Vivian Girls over a vast nation of girl warriors—and Darger's desire (as

MacGregor has argued) of being adopted by a gang of little girls—may look less strange when one considers the extensive and fully public discussion of general female supereminence carried on by such a highly respectable authority as William Moulton Marston in the mass middlebrow press (as well as in the lowbrow comics realm) during the years leading up to and during the Second World War. How could the man who claimed to have invented the lie detector be speaking anything but the truth? But the efforts of a few people like Marston did not succeed in moving the figure of the woman or girl from the generally abject (although occasionally supereminent) place to which she tended to be consigned in male-authored and male-directed pulp of the early and mid-twentieth century. Indeed, as we have seen in earlier pulp, as we do in Darger's work, the occasional supereminence of a female figure or of a small number of them is routinely accompanied by an otherwise generalized female abjection.

In the closing section of this chapter, I want to look more closely at the strains of misogynistic cruelty (and envy, fear, and loathing of the feminine) that continued to manifest itself in US mass culture in the post-pulp period. The popular novelist Robert Bloch, the author of *Psycho*, is a key figure in this connection. Bloch was a leading mass-market writer in the last years of the pulp period and after, as the new publishing phenomenon of the comic book, especially the superhero comic, drew away much of the pulp magazines' target audiences of young men and boys—as we have just seen in the case of the *Wonder Woman* comics. Like a number of other teenage devotees of *Weird Tales* in the 1930s, Bloch had sent Lovecraft a fan letter and subsequently developed a close epistolary friendship with him. Bloch soon entered into a literary apprenticeship with the older man that involved him in developing his own as well as some of Lovecraft's distinctive narrative materials (Bloch soon became a notable producer of "Cthulhu Mythos" tales). In what must have been a particularly delicate set of negotiations in cross-generational power relations, Lovecraft and Bloch gave each other permission to kill off characters based on each other in two of their respective publications. Lovecraft died in March 1937, shortly before Bloch's twentieth birthday. In the ensuing decade, Bloch succeeded Lovecraft as one of the most popular contributors to *Weird Tales*, with his work often appearing next to that of another of his elders, Seabury Quinn.

A subsequent work of Bloch's, his 1959 novel *Psycho*—its pulp elements firmly intact—would, in its adaptation for the screen by Alfred Hitchcock, take the rank misogyny that we sometimes see in pulp fiction, and in Darger's private fiction of the 1920s and 1930s, to quite a different place. Both the novel and the book would also be extremely influential in establishing a new focus for both acts and fantasies of extreme violence, often although not always against women, through the late-twentieth-century cult of the serial killer. This popular fascination with serial-killer figures, images, and narratives would in turn be highly significant in the reception of Darger's art and writing in the decade after his work first hit the mainstream, in the late 1990s.

A series of sensational arrests and trials in the late 1970s—of David Berkowitz ("Son of Sam"), Ted Bundy, John Wayne Gacy Jr., and others— and a long, still ongoing series of very popular books and films about multiple murders and killing sprees have kept the figure of the serial killer at the center of attention in both news media and popular commercial films for the past three decades. Behind several of the most influential slasher or serial-killer fictions of the second half of the twentieth century, from *Psycho* to *Silence of the Lambs* and *American Psycho*, stands an earlier, less-well-remembered figure from the 1950s named Ed Gein. The story of Gein's childhood unfolds with a terrible kind of familiarity. The son of a violent and alcoholic father and a fanatically religious mother determined to "save" Ed and his older brother, Henry, from sin and corruption by isolating them on the family farm, Ed was dominated by his mother. That fact, his effeminate manner, a slight facial deformity, and a tendency to laugh quietly for no reason apparent to anyone else made him an outcast at school. As an adult, he was regarded by the rural Wisconsin community where the Geins lived as a harmless oddball. Besides working alongside his brother on the family farm, Ed was often called on to babysit various neighbors' children, other adults having noticed that he seemed more at ease in the company of children. Ed's passage into early middle age was marked by the deaths of the other members of his own family: his father in 1940 (when Ed was thirty-four), his brother in 1944, and his mother the following year. Ed lived on in the family farmhouse, subsisting financially on what he earned from doing odd jobs. Besides doing a minimal amount of grocery shopping, he was known by his fellow villagers to spend some of his meager funds on pulp magazines of the "weird tale" and "amazing adventure" varieties.

Ed Gein continued to lead his solitary life on the farm for twelve years after his mother's death, until a November day in 1957, when local police came to investigate the disappearance of the woman who owned and ran the local hardware store. They found her corpse hanging in a shed on Gein's property, "dressed out" the way hunters prepare deer they have shot. Searching the house, the police discovered a macabre assortment of domestic furnishings (lampshades, windowshade pulls, cups, and bowls) and articles of clothing (vest, belt, socks) made of human skin and bones. Most disturbing of all was the discovery of two caches of objects, one fabricated from the flesh of human faces and the other from female external genitalia, both of which Gein had tanned into prostheses that he admitted to "wearing." Gein had obtained the body parts from the corpses of his recent murder victim, from another woman he had murdered three years earlier, and from robbing graves. The police said that Gein looked for the bodies of women whom he thought resembled his late mother in some way.

The publicity accorded these grisly discoveries continued to resonate widely and recurrently in and beyond the United States for decades thereafter. When Gein's crimes were first discovered, Robert Bloch was living in rural Wisconsin, just a county away from the scene of Gein's murders and grave robberies. Bloch's *Psycho*, published less than two years after the revelation of Gein's crimes, was one of the first mass-circulated narratives to depict and to some degree to try to explain gruesome and extremely violent behavior like Gein's. Bloch's proximity to the scene of Gein's crimes may have contributed to his book's eventual status as a canonical statement of the disquieting perception (chillingly affirmed by the appearance in 1966 of Truman Capote's *In Cold Blood*, about the 1959 murder of a family in rural Kansas) that a farmhouse down the road in the heartland may become the scene of atrocious crimes.

Hitchcock's celebrated 1960 film *Psycho* adds its own set of weird and disturbing images (most unforgettably, the stabbing murder of the female protagonist in the shower) to the set of uncanny objects and relations that Bloch had appropriated for his novel from print accounts of Gein's story and that Hitchcock adapts for his film, such as the intense devotion toward (and identification with) the domineering (and deceased) mother that the son feels, and the evidence of his skill at his "hobby" of taxidermy in the stuffed animals on display in his dining room. Hitchcock's casting of the young Anthony Perkins as the "psycho," Norman Bates, has been generally regarded as a marked departure from the facts of the case on which the narrative is based: far from resembling a lissome young Hollywood leading man, the Gein whose picture appeared in the papers in 1957 was a rather scruffy-looking fifty-year-old cast in the recognizable mold of poor rural loner and strange old man. Yet in casting in the role an actor who was just beginning to outgrow the *ingénu* persona that had made him a star, Hitchcock may have been preserving in the most highly visible way he could the edge of perversion and ordinary or everyday forbiddenness that may have attached to the less sensational aspects of Gein's story: the facts that he had been an effeminate boy and young man who enjoyed babysitting and child care and that he was dominated by his evil or crazy mother—even (or especially) after her death. Obviously, the elements of effeminacy and of an elaborate maternal identification in various manifestations closely fit a pervasive 1950s stereotype of the homosexual. The reason that Hitchcock himself gave for casting Perkins in the role was to make the Norman Bates character more sympathetic to audiences by embodying the character in an actor who supposedly possessed in spades what the director characterized as Perkins's boy-next-door looks and manner.[23] In casting Perkins, who was one of several preternaturally beautiful young Hollywood actors of the period whose closetedness spoke thunderously silent volumes about everyday forbidden erotic desire and drive in the period (their numbers also included Rock Hudson, Tab Hunter, and Montgomery Clift), Hitchcock was able to do what virtually no one else has been able to do in retelling Ed Gein's story: to keep alive in the reader or viewer a kernel not only of sympathetic identification with the character, but also of sympathy with his desire.

A considerably less sympathetic version of the story of Gein's crimes was told in another enormously popular and influential film, *The Texas Chainsaw Massacre* (1974). What is preserved in this version of the story from elements of the publicity around Gein's case is the gothic element of rural isolation and the single sensational detail of the masks made of skin from human faces, worn in this narrative by the chainsaw-wielding Leatherface. The solitary figure of Gein is multiplied in this version of the story into an entire family of rural cannibalistic killers. Other elements of Gein's story figure centrally in Thomas Harris's 1988 novel and Jonathan Demme's 1991 film of *Silence of the Lambs*, in which the serial killer "Buffalo Bill" composes a "woman suit" of parts of women's bodies he has dissected and preserved. By the time Bret Easton Ellis published *American Psycho* in 1991, his satirical novel about a 1980s Wall Street yuppy serial killer, the gesture toward Bloch's and Hitchcock's *Psycho* was to be expected, as were the blithely murderous narrator's offhand references to Ed Gein. All that is carried on from the Gein narrative is the element of its rank misogyny: the hyperviolent destruction of women's lives and bodies (in Gein's case), apparently to fashion a wardrobe of fetishistic accoutrements in which he can "dress up" (right down to wearing "her" genitals) as his late mother.

In trying to understand the significance of the violence against little girls' bodies that is a recurrent feature of Darger's work and to interpret it for his own readers, MacGregor turns to several popular forensic "profilers" of serial killers, chiefly the self-proclaimed "Monster-Fighter for the FBI," Robert K. Ressler (the coauthor, with Tom Shachtman, of *Whoever Fights Monsters: My Twenty Years Tracking Serial Killers for the FBI*, 1992) and Helen Morrison (the coauthor, with Harold Goldberg, of *My Life among the Serial Killers*, 2004). Anyone who reads such books with even a little knowledge of modern popular fiction will soon be struck by the preponderance of readily recognizable pulp motifs, images, and character types in work that presents itself to the reader as supposedly authoritative and scientific. Although it does seem to be the case that Ed Gein passed many of his lonely hours alone on the family farm reading "weird" pulps, all of us who have watched television or gone to movies in recent decades (and this would certainly include MacGregor's serial-killer profilers) are more or less steeped in many of the ruling clichés of "weird" pulp fiction. Gein's atrocious crimes, of course, can't simply be blamed on his penchant for pulp fiction. Nor can the features of Darger's mind as MacGregor sees it reflected in some of his work—his work at its most violent—be sufficiently or satisfactorily illuminated by the conceptual vocabulary and language of a few profilers who themselves trade largely in the conceptual vocabulary of monstrous and monster-fighting pulp fiction. What may look to the uninformed reader or viewer of some of Darger's work like the bizarre, perhaps even unique, aberration of a deeply disturbed individual is actually part of a highly crafted record of a set of weird fantasies explored in writing and painting to a remarkably thorough degree, which in their very extremity manifest their intimate relatedness to some of the most widely disseminated, and widely disavowed, sets of fantasies of twentieth-century males. The more we study the most popular fiction of the twentieth century, the more we see that it is in what have been generally taken to be some of its most outré features that Darger's work most tellingly betrays its kinship with some of the most everyday fantasies of the ordinary man, the self-proclaimed regular guy of the twentieth century.

How weird was Henry Darger? Was he crazy, or just eccentric? Was he insane, as the form admitting him to the Lincoln Home for Feebleminded Children alleged he was, and as some students of his work today believe he must have been (by his own account, "Crazy" had been his nickname in elementary school)? Surely it would be a genuinely quixotic project to try at this point to establish his sanity or insanity. I prefer to think of him as having been in some ways very productively unreasonable in the way he conducted his life, relentlessly producing art and writing out of sight of other people for five or six decades. But this out-of-sightness that was the condition of his sixty years of ceaseless creative labor was by no means simply a space of isolation and privation; the space in which he imagined and executed his work may turn out to have been, if we can bring ourselves to see it as such, an eminently public and political space, albeit only after Darger's death.

In thinking about the place of "unreason" in the so-called Classical Age of Reason, Michel Foucault hypothesized that "unreason would be the long memory of peoples, their greatest fidelity to the past."[24] Darger, I believe, was possessed of (and perhaps also by) just such a "long memory" as Foucault attributes to "peoples" in the mass—a memory, indeed, that may have been much longer than he realized. Through his lifelong involvement in producing fantasy, writing, and art about the everyday and extreme sufferings of some children, little girls, religious and political martyrs to noble causes, noncombatants in war, and the class of slaves, Darger can be seen as having enacted a great "fidelity to the past"—to an indeterminate number of pasts, some of which extend back to the Civil War and others of which may extend even further back, to the Wars of Religion and the Reformation and Counter-Reformation in Europe. These pasts also include (if often in only highly fragmentary and occluded traces) a number of other pasts that have only recently made their way into academic discourses of history: the pasts of children, girls and women, and other such subaltern populations as the insane and the perverted. Part of Darger's "fidelity" may adhere in the way any serious consideration of his work inevitably brings viewers and readers into the highly toxic vicinity of acts and scenes of atrocity that most of us prefer not to dwell on. Darger lived for the last half of his life at 851 Webster Avenue, in the Lincoln Park section of Chicago. One of Emily Dickinson's poems begins by making the claim, "I dwell in Possibility, / A fairer house than prose." Darger the artist, proletarian aesthete, and imaginative forger, chronicler, and limner of "what is known as the realms of the unreal," in contrast dwelled in Necessity—and judging from his work, in a prolonged state of "dwelling on," or being preternaturally attuned to, the historical reality and extrahistorical excess ("beyond reality," "in the realms of the unreal") of atrocity and its effects on perpetrators, victims, and survivors. Given that, aren't we blaming the messenger when we try to attribute to some personal deformation of Darger's own the toxicity and horror with which his work sometimes brings us into too close contact?

NOTES

Preface

1 Quoted in Gombrich, *Aby Warburg*, 108.
2 Here I am referring in general to Walter Benjamin, *The Arcades Project*, and specifically to its opening section, "Paris, the Capital of the Nineteenth Century," including Benjamin's discussion of Baudelaire, which appears on pp. 10–11 and 21–23.

Introduction

1 Oskar Negt and Alexander Kluge present their version of a proletarian public sphere, one that had considerable autonomy in relation to the bourgeois public sphere (which had been theorized a little earlier by Jürgen Habermas) with which it also overlapped, in *Public Sphere and Experience*. Miriam Hansen begins the task of conceptually translating and refining some of Negt and Kluge's leading ideas into an analysis of early cinema as proletarian public sphere in "Early Cinema, Late Cinema" and other articles. Somewhat less systematic but nonetheless similarly enlightening and stimulating has been some of the scholarly work on the respective audiences for the early newspaper comic strip, proletarian fiction, and the performance styles of African American, Native American, and Popular Front musicians. Work like George Chauncey's on the social history and interactions of various communities of queers in New York City around the beginning of the twentieth century adds another indispensable dimension to the still-forming picture of the myriad interacting sectors of the US urban proletarian public sphere a hundred years ago. Franklin Rosemont and his colleagues in the Chicago surrealist movement have also done important service in preserving the products and memory of the intersections of "hobohemian" culture, "outsider art," and antiwar and anticapitalist organizing in Darger's native city (see Rosemont, *Surrealism and Its Popular Accomplices*).

2 As I shall discuss in more detail in my chapter on Darger and pulp fiction and painting, Carlo Rotella's "Pulp History" was helpful to me in initially recognizing the relation of Darger's work to pulp narrative and "pulp history." Rotella's account of some leading authors of now-classic pulp fiction, such as Robert E. Howard (of "Conan" fame), and their fidelity in their writing to various historical lost causes and foreclosed futures, seems to me highly resonant with some of the emphases of Darger's often melancholy and violent narratives.

3 John M. MacGregor discusses Darger's friendship with Schloeder, Schloeder's many appearances as a character in Darger's writing, and his possible knowledge of Darger's work in the invaluable long biographical first chapter on the artist in MacGregor, *Henry Darger*, 62–65. Michael Bonesteel has also done important biographical research on Darger; see Bonesteel, "Henry Darger, Author, Artist, Sorry Saint, Protector of Children," 7–35.

4 Williams, *Playing the Race Card*.

5 Darger's work, exceptional in so many other ways, is of a piece with that of other sentimental white writers about slavery in its general obliviousness to the persons and histories of nonwhite populations—the only characters from *Uncle Tom's Cabin* in whom he appears to take an active interest are Little Eva and her father. Both his writing and drawing focus exclusively on white heroism; African American characters appear only once in a great while in the saga (and only in the written parts), and even then in the most conventional roles of body servants to their white masters. But unlike D. W. Griffith, his contemporary who championed the Klan, Darger's Yankee sympathies (after all, he never left his native Illinois) are apparent in his recurrent association of various signs of the Confederacy with his Glandelinian "bad guys."

6 For a collection of innovative analyses of "vast narratives" (including Darger's) in various media throughout the course of the twentieth century, see Harrigan and Wardrip-Fruin, *Third Person*.

7 Two photographs of a young Darger with Schloeder are reproduced in MacGregor, *Henry Darger*, 63.

8 Moon, "The Gentle Boy from the Dangerous Classes."

9 Quoted in MacGregor, *Henry Darger*, 265.

10 The story has been told repeatedly of how Darger's actual loss of a photograph of a little girl named Elsie Paroubek, who had been kidnapped and whose body was subsequently found, seems to have set off an intense and obsessive response on his part that came to permeate his writing of *In the Realms*. Bonesteel did some of the earliest research on this; see his "Henry Darger: Author, Artist, Sorry Saint, Protector of Children," 10–11. In *In the Realms*, one of the numerous characters named "Darger" loses a photograph of the girl martyr Annie Aronburg, a loss that gives rise to the so-called Aronburg Mystery. I will discuss this in some detail in chapter 1.

11 Pop-narrative scholars have long recognized that in having the boy Tip turn into Princess Ozma at the dramatic climax of *The Marvelous Land of Oz*, Baum was drawing directly on one of the key moments in the enormously popular tradition of the grand fairy pantomime (from which today's Christmas panto is descended), in which the principal boy, usually played by a leggy young female star, is magically transformed from a boy into a young woman near the end of the narrative, at the same time that the ordinary or squalid surroundings on the stage are magically transformed into fairyland.

12 See, for example, Baum's characterization of the "modernized fairy tale" in his preface to *The Wonderful Wizard of Oz*, ed. Susan Wolstenholme, 3–4.

13 MacGregor writes: "Given the fact that all the girls in *The Realms* possess male genitals, how is anyone to know [what 'sex' a given person is]?" (*Henry Darger*, 266).

14 I heartily thank J. Keith Vincent and Dawn Lawson for making available to me their translation of Saitō's *Beautiful Fighting Girl*.

15 On Saitō's discussion of the otaku's quest for "an autonomous object," see his *Beautiful Fighting Girl*, 151, and on Darger's drive to imbue his work with an "autonomous reality," see *Beautiful Fighting Girl*, 167. Besides his sympathetic defense of otaku sexuality, Saitō has also published an important and influential book analyzing another antisocial phenomenon that troubles many Japanese: large numbers of young people who refuse to leave their rooms at home, often for extended periods of time. Again, Saitō points to Darger's lifelong project of turning his small room into an alternate world as an interesting anticipation of what has become in contemporary Japan and elsewhere a widespread phenomenon and alleged social problem. See Maggie Jones, "Shutting Themselves In," *New York Times Magazine*, January 15, 2006.

16 Riley, *Oz and Beyond*, 202–29.

17 MacGregor, *Henry Darger*, 226.

18 MacGregor is quoted as saying: "Psychologically, Darger was undoubtedly a serial killer," and then opining, "I don't think he acted, however, because if he'd ever started, he wouldn't have been able to stop. Instead he sublimated it into his art." See Tessa DeCarlo, "The Bizarre Visions of a Reclusive Master," *New York Times*, January 12, 1997. On MacGregor's subsequent rediagnosis of Darger, see "Appendix A: On the Problem of Diagnosis," in his *Henry Darger*.

19 MacGregor, *Henry Darger*, 224–26.

20 As the son of a German immigrant, Darger may have heard tales of children's heroism and spectacular suffering in wartime that extend back in oral tradition as well as in print to the Thirty Years' War (1618–48). Johann Grimmelshausen's *Simplicissimus*, as revolutionary in its effects on early modern German fiction as Bunyan's (and Defoe's) writings were on English narrative or Cervantes's on Spanish, presents a world that does not seem very remote from Darger's. At the age of ten, Grimmelshausen had himself been kidnapped by hostile soldiers and may

have observed many of the kinds of atrocities he relates in the long-popular *Simplicissimus*. The authors of several different narratives of children's experience in the Shoah (whether presented as authentic memoirs or as fictionalized autobiography) have been the object of highly publicized accusations of both substantially fabricating and plagiarizing their accounts, from Jerzy Kosinski's *The Painted Bird* (1965) to the debunked memoirs of Binjamin Wilkomirski and Herman Rosenblat. The authoring of atrocity narratives about the alleged experiences of children in wartime has clearly been a highly charged practice for some time, and the near-complete secrecy in which Darger worked may have been at least in part a strategic response to the risk involved in writing (not to mention drawing and painting scenes from) such narratives. The figure of the child soldier and the child survivor of atrocities—often figured as African children being rescued by American humanitarians—is currently in very wide circulation in the United States, as the success of a series of recently published memoirs, novels (such as Dave Eggers's *What Is the What*), documentary films, and episodes of television series about the so-called lost boys of Sudan all attest.

21 MacGregor, *Henry Darger*, figure 7.19.

22 Ibid., figure 8.6.

23 Bonesteel, "Henry Darger: Author, Artist, Sorry Saint, Protector of Children," 17.

24 Schwartz, "The Suspended Moment," 21. A reproduction of the painting appears in MacGregor, *Henry Darger*, figure 12.3.

25 MacGregor, *Henry Darger*, figure 12.3.

26 A reproduction of the painting titled *They Were Almost Murdered Themselves* appears in ibid., figure 11.21.

27 Ibid., figure 11.7.

28 MacGregor writes that it was in his panoramic paintings that Darger could "be a little girl among [other] little girls," and that these images functioned primarily as "environments" he made for himself to enjoy and inhabit rather than as "pictures" or paintings more conventionally conceived as works of art produced for others (ibid., 342).

29 The concept of the half-real seems a promising one for thinking about Darger's work and about the problematics and erotics of fantasy in general. See, for example, Jesper Juul's elaboration of the concept in relation to the history and theory of games in *Half-Real*.

30 Sakolsky, "Introduction," 95–96. Also in Sakolsky's volume, see Joseph Jablonski's important early (1979) essay on Darger, "Henry J. Darger," which also appears in Rosemont, *Surrealism and Its Popular Accomplices*, 101–2.

1   The full run of *Treasure Chest* comics is available online at http://archives.lib.cua
    .edu/findingaid/treasurechest.cfm#series1 as a service of the American Catho-
    lic History Research Center at the Catholic University of America. The story I'm
    discussing appears in *Treasure Chest* 10, no. 10 (January 13, 1954). The comic had
    run two previous features on the martyrdom of the thirteen-year-old saint, in
    1947 and 1950. The 1954 feature is conspicuously gorier than the earlier two. That
    same year, Fredric Wertham's book *Seduction of the Innocent* and the ensuing public
    debate about the depiction of extreme physical violence as well as the allegedly
    "perverse" sexual subtexts of "crime comics" led to the institution of the Comics
    Code and the supposed banishment of violence, gore, and (even mild) kink in
    any form from comics. Clearly, the virgin-torture scenarios of religious comics of
    the time were exempted from public consideration for a long time thereafter. For
    the beginning of a public response from the comics underground to the ethos of
    parochial-school education before the Second Vatican Council, see Justin Green's
    pioneering 1972 autobiographical comic "Binky Brown Meets the Holy Virgin."

2   McDannell, *Material Christianity*, 170. Subsequent page-number references to this
    book are given in parentheses in the text.

3   Enders, *The Medieval Theater of Cruelty*, 192–93. See also 192–202.

4   Ibid., 192–93.

5   See, for example, Egginton, *How the World Became a Stage*, 54.

6   See, for example, the entries "Pornography" (by Thomas Hägg, p. 648) and
    "Nudity" (by Megan Reid, pp. 615–16) in Bowersock, Brown, and Grabar, *Late An-
    tiquity*.

7   MacGregor gives the story of Jenny Anges in *Henry Darger*, 633–34. All quotations
    in my account of the story are from these pages. For this episode, MacGregor
    cites the manuscripts of *In the Realms*, 9:884b–85.

8   Quoted in Elsky, "Introduction to Erich Auerbach," 287.

9   MacGregor devotes an entire chapter of his *Henry Darger* to exploring "The Aron-
    burg Mystery." Subsequent references to material he quotes from *In the Realms* ap-
    pear in parentheses in the present text.

10 See, for example, Scheper-Hughes, "The Global Traffic in Organs"; and Casta-
    ñeda's chapter "Rumored Realities: Child-Organ Theft," in her book, *Figurations*,
    110–41.

11 On the politics of martyrdom in the contemporary world, see Mack, "Editor's
    Introduction."

12 Benjamin, *The Origin of German Tragic Drama*.

13 Given the importance to Darger and his project of two of the other great self-
    sequelating fictions of the seventeenth century, *Don Quixote* and *Pilgrim's Progress*,

one may wonder if in his wide reading Darger ever ran across Johann Grimmelshausen's *Simplicissimus*, the German counterpart to these texts, in which a naive narrator recounts his endless misadventures from childhood on, amid the atmosphere of atrocity and mass death that pervades his war-torn homeland. The author, like Benjamin's Gryphius, had been orphaned and dislocated in the Thirty Years' War as a child, and had experienced the subjection of his own and other people to grotesque violence at close range from a very early age. Like the Mitchell translation in the bibliography, Walter Wallich's 1962 translation is highly readable.

14 The critic David Krasner has inaugurated the difficult and important work of "translating" Benjamin's analysis of the baroque mourning-play into US, African American, and Native American historical contexts in "Walter Benjamin and the Lynching Play."

2. Rotten Truths, Wasted Lives

1 See, for example, Markus, "Realms of the Unreal." See also Warner, "Out of an Old Toy Chest."

2 On the Brontës' absorptive reading of *Blackwood's*, see Alexander, *The Early Writings of Charlotte Brontë*, 20. The analogy between the images of atrocity in Goya's *Disasters of War* etchings and some of Darger's images of torture and martyrdom was powerfully made by Klaus Biesenbach's exhibition, "Disasters of War," which juxtaposed work by the two artists. The exhibition was at the P.S.1 Contemporary Art Center in Long Island City, Queens, from November 2000 through March 2001.

3 Barker, *The Brontës*, 155. My account of the emergence of the Brontës' juvenilia from their toy-soldier "plays" depends throughout on Barker's biography and on Alexander's introduction to her *Early Writings of Charlotte Brontë*.

4 Alexander, *Early Writings of Charlotte Brontë*, 96.

5 Barker, *The Brontës*, 154 and 864, note 53.

6 Quoted in Alexander, *Early Writings of Charlotte Brontë*, 199.

7 P. Brontë, *The Works of Patrick Branwell Brontë*.

8 Brown, "Beloved Objects."

9 C. Brontë, "The History of the Year," in *The Glass Town Saga*, 4.

10 Ibid., 5.

11 Quoted in Brown, "Beloved Objects," 412.

12 Ibid.; Brown borrows the phrase "absurd satisfaction" from Octave Mannoni.

13 P. Brontë, *The Works of Patrick Branwell Brontë*, 1:138.

14 Alexander, *Early Writings of Charlotte Brontë*, 30.

15 Ibid., 38.

16 Ibid.

17 MacGregor, *Henry Darger*, 681, note 75.

18 Michael Bonesteel discusses the charges that were made against physicians and other staff members at the Lincoln Asylum during Darger's residence there in his "Henry Darger: Author, Artist, Sorry Saint, Protector of Children," 9.

19 Alexander, *Early Writings of Charlotte Brontë*, 34.

20 Ibid., 86.

21 Kiyoko Lerner tells this story in Jessica Yu's documentary *In the Realms of the Unreal* (2004).

22 Brooke Davis Anderson reported this to me in a conversation in April 2004.

23 MacGregor, *Henry Darger*, 117.

24 Gaskell, *The Letters of Mrs. Gaskell*, 398.

25 Daphne du Maurier, "Second Thoughts on Branwell," *Brontë Society Transactions* 23, no. 2 (October 1998): 156.

26 For a succinct statement of Klein's early thinking about infant aggression, see the entries "Aggression, Sadism and Component Instincts" and "Babies" in R. D. Hinshelwood, *A Dictionary of Kleinian Thought* (Northvale, NJ: Jason Aronson, 1991), 46–56 and 225–26, respectively.

27 MacGregor, *Henry Darger*, 58.

28 Gérin, *Branwell Brontë*, 34–35.

29 Ibid., 78.

30 Patrick Branwell Brontë, *The Works of Patrick Branwell Brontë*, ed. Victor A. Neufeldt (New York: Garland, 1997), 1:139, note 7.

31 Ibid., 1:139.

32 Ibid., 1:140–41.

33 Ibid., 2:278.

34 Ibid., 2:302–3.

35 Ibid., 3:303.

36 Ibid., 3:445.

37 Ibid., 2:603.

38 Ibid., 1:212, note 3.

39 Quoted in MacGregor, *Henry Darger*, 115.

40 Mooney, *The Ghost-Dance Religion and the Sioux Outbreak of 1890*, 322.

41 Quoted in MacGregor, *Henry Darger*, 374.

42 Ibid., 377.

43 Quoted in ibid., 703, note 107.

44 Ibid., 541.

45 Ibid., 702, note 14.

46 Ibid., 703, note 96.

47 Ibid., 45.

48 Tessa DeCarlo, "The Bizarre Visions of a Reclusive Master," *New York Times*, January 12, 1997.

49 MacGregor, *Henry Darger: In the Realms of the Unreal*, 45.

50 See du Maurier, *The Infernal World of Branwell Brontë*, 52–53.

51 Ibid., 215.

52 P. Brontë, *The Works of Patrick Branwell Brontë*, 2:365.

53 Alexander and Sellars, *The Art of the Brontës*, 347.

54 P. Brontë, *The Works of Patrick Branwell Brontë*, 2:558.

55 Santner, *My Own Private Germany*, 10.

56 MacGregor, *Henry Darger*, 680, note 344.

57 Quoted in ibid., 84.

3. Abduction, Adoption, Appropriation

1 MacGregor, *Henry Darger*, 269.

2 Gordon tells the story in rich detail in *The Great Arizona Orphan Abduction*.

3 Negt and Kluge, *Public Sphere and Experience*.

4 Miriam Hansen's extensive work on the early cinema has been instrumental in making it an important site for the critical exploration of Negt and Kluge's theories of the proletarian public sphere, and for critiquing some of the limitations of these theories. See, for example, Hansen, "Early Cinema, Late Cinema."

5 MacGregor, *Henry Darger*, 678, note 250.

6 Nelson, *Little Strangers*.

7 See Horn, *One Hundred Years of American Newspaper Comics*, 178.

8 The comics historian Maurice Horn says that, at the outset, Little Annie Rooney was "a feisty, belligerent moppet" like her original, Little Orphan Annie, but that the distributing syndicate decided that merely trying to clone Annie was not likely to attract as many fans as maximizing the pathos of Little Annie Rooney's situation might. See ibid.

9 See MacGregor's discussion of Darger's use of "Mr. Mutt and Mr. Jeff" in his *Henry Darger*, 251–52.

10 Robert Harvey recounts the early history of *Mutt and Jeff* in detail in *The Art of the Funnies*, 35–47.

11 Quoted in MacGregor, *Henry Darger*, 252.

12 Quoted in Harvey, *The Art of the Funnies*, 47.

13 Seldes, *The Seven Lively Arts*, 218, 224.

14 Carlo Rotella, "Pulp History," *Raritan* 27, no. 1 (Summer 2007): 11–36.

4. Weird Flesh, World's Flesh

1 Merleau-Ponty, *The Visible and the Invisible*, 248.

2 Ibid., 268.

3 For a brilliant reassessment of the significance of Lovecraft's writing, see Michel

Houellebecq's 1991 book, translated into English as H. P. Lovecraft: Against the World, against Life.

4 Walt Whitman, "Song of Myself," in *Leaves of Grass and Other Writings*, ed. Michael Moon (New York: Norton, 2002), section 51, 77.

5 H. P. Lovecraft, *Tales*, compiled by Peter Straub from texts edited by S.T. Joshi (New York: Library of America, 2005), 167.

6 The first National Amateur Press Association was organized in Philadelphia and held its first conference in 1876; it is still an active organization (see http://www .amateurpress.org/). The entire first volume of Lovecraft's *Collected Essays* (440 pages of text, called *Amateur Journalism*) is devoted to his writings about amateur writing and presses. In a piece in the volume, "What Amateurdom and I Have Done for Each Other," Lovecraft writes: "What I have given Amateur Journalism is regrettably little; what Amateur Journalism has given me is—life itself" (273).

7 See Yu's documentary *In the Realms of the Unreal*.

8 L. Sprague de Camp in association with Catherine Crook de Camp and Jane Whittington Griffin, *Dark Valley Destiny: The Life of Robert E. Howard* (New York: St. Martin's, 1986). Mark Finn offers a corrective to what he sees as de Camp's over-emphasis on the Oedipal in his *Blood and Thunder: The Life and Art of Robert E. Howard* (Austin, TX: MonkeyBrain Books, 2006).

9 Literary critics and cultural historians have so far paid little attention to the question of what pulp magazines of various kinds may have meant to their respective audiences. A notable exception to this pattern is Erin A. Smith, who attempts to relate working-class male concerns about shifting standards of masculine achievement in consumer society to the hard-boiled-detective subgenre of 1930s pulp magazines. See Smith, *Hard-Boiled*.

10 See the entries on "Aggression, Sadism and Component Instincts" and "Babies" in R. D. Hinshelwood, *A Dictionary of Kleinian Thought* (Northvale, NJ: Jason Aronson, 1991), 46–56 and 225–26, respectively.

11 Rotella, "Pulp History," 11.

12 Ibid., 16.

13 Ibid.

14 Ibid., 19–20.

15 For one of the most intellectually productive engagements with Freud's Jewishness and the character of psychoanalysis as a "Jewish science," see Jacques Derrida, *Mal d'archive* (translated into English as *Archive Fever*).

16 Jerry Siegel and Joe Schuster started circulating the material that became Superman comics in 1934, when they were both twenty, and saw it take off as a popular, nationally circulated publication in 1938. Geoff Klock reads superhero comics in a psychoanalytic context highly mediated by Harold Bloom, in *How to Read Superhero Comics and Why*. Danny Fingeroth relates mid-century American Jewish identities to the emergence of superhero comics in his *Disguised as Clark Kent*.

17 Brundage deserves her own entry in the annals of homegrown Chicago surrealism, both for her girl-on-girl bondage-and-discipline art and her marriage in the 1920s and 1930s, when she was one of *Weird Tales*'s key contributors, to the "hobohemian" anarchist Myron "Slim" Brundage, whose *Selected Ravings* were posthumously edited and published by Franklin Rosemont, the doyen of later-twentieth-century Chicago surrealism whom we encountered in the introduction.

18 Anderson, "The Crucified Woman."

19 Seabury Quinn, *Alien Flesh* (Philadelphia: O. Train, 1977), 95.

20 Ibid., 231.

21 My account of the contretemps caused by this letter depends on Bunn, "The Lie Detector," which quotes the sergeant's and Gaines's letters on page 94.

22 Quoted in ibid., 111.

23 Joseph Stefano, who wrote the screenplay for *Psycho*, has spoken in interviews since about his initial lack of sympathy for the Norman Bates character and Hitchcock's idea of making the character seem attractive by casting Anthony Perkins in the role; see Stephen Rebello, *Alfred Hitchcock and the Making of Psycho* (New York: St. Martin's, 1998), 39.

24 Quoted in Eribon, *Michel Foucault*, 118.

BIBLIOGRAPHY

Agamben, Giorgio. *Ninfe*. Torino: Bollati Boringhieri, 2007.

Alexander, Christine. *The Early Writings of Charlotte Brontë*. Buffalo, NY: Prometheus, 1983.

Alexander, Christine, and Jane Sellars. *The Art of the Brontës*. Cambridge: Cambridge University Press, 1995.

Anderson, Rachel. "The Crucified Woman: A Paradox of Prurience and Piety," May 21, 2007. Unpublished paper, University of Washington (https://dlib.lib.washington .edu/dspace/bitstream/handle/1773/3101/anderson_project.pdf?sequence=1).

Barker, Juliet. *The Brontës*. New York: St. Martin's, 1994.

Benjamin, Walter. *The Arcades Project*. Translated by Howard Eiland and Kevin McLaughlin. Cambridge: Harvard University, 1999.

———. *The Origin of German Tragic Drama*. Translated by John Osborne. London: New Left, 1977.

Bonesteel, Michael. "Henry Darger: Author, Artist, Sorry Saint, Protector of Children." In *Henry Darger: Art and Selected Writings*, edited by Michael Bonesteel, 5–35. New York: Rizzoli, 2000.

———. "Henry Darger's Search for the Grail in the Guise of a Celestial Child." In *Third Person: Authoring and Exploring Vast Narratives*, edited by Pat Harrigan and Noah Wardrip-Fruin, 253–65. Cambridge: MIT Press, 2009.

Bowersock, G. W., Peter Brown, and Oleg Grabar, eds. *Late Antiquity: A Guide to the Postclassical World*. Cambridge: Harvard University Press, 1999.

Brontë, Charlotte. *The Glass Town Saga, 1826–1832*. Vol. 1 of *An Edition of the Early Writings of Charlotte Brontë*. Edited by Christine Alexander. New York: Basil Blackwell, 1987.

Brontë, Patrick Branwell. *The Works of Patrick Branwell Brontë*. Edited by Victor A. Neufeldt. 3 vols. New York: Garland, 1997–99.

Brown, Kate. "Beloved Objects: Mourning, Materiality, and Charlotte Brontë's 'Never-Ending Story.'" ELH 65, no. 2 (1998): 395–421.

Bunn, Geoffrey C. "The Lie Detector, *Wonder Woman* and Liberty: The Life and Work of William Moulton Marston." *History of the Human Sciences* 10, no. 1 (1997): 91–119.

Castañeda, Claudia. *Figurations: Child, Bodies, Worlds.* Durham: Duke University Press, 2002.

Derrida, Jacques. *Archive Fever.* Translated by Eric Prenowitz. Chicago: University of Chicago Press, 1996.

———. "The Violence of the Letter." In *Of Grammatology*, 111–12. Corrected ed. Translated by Gayatri Chakravorty Spivak. Baltimore: The Johns Hopkins University Press, 1998.

Du Maurier, Daphne. *The Infernal World of Branwell Brontë.* New York: Doubleday, 1960.

Egginton, William. *How the World Became a Stage.* Albany: State University of New York Press, 2003.

Elsky, Martin. "Introduction to Erich Auerbach, '*Passio* as Passion.'" *Criticism* 43, no. 3 (2001): 285–90.

Enders, Jody. *The Medieval Theater of Cruelty: Rhetoric, Memory, Violence.* Ithaca: Cornell University Press, 1992.

Eribon, Didier. *Michel Foucault.* Translated by Betsy Wing. Cambridge: Harvard University Press, 1991.

Fingeroth, Danny. *Disguised as Clark Kent: Jews, Comics, and the Creation of the Superhero.* New York: Continuum, 2007.

Gaskell, Elizabeth. *The Letters of Mrs. Gaskell.* Edited by J. A. V. Chappel and Arthur Pollard. Manchester, UK: University of Manchester Press, 1997.

Gérin, Winifred. *Branwell Brontë.* London: Thomas Nelson, 1961.

Gombrich, E. H. *Aby Warburg: An Intellectual Biography.* 2nd ed. Oxford: Phaidon, 1986.

Gordon, Linda. *The Great Arizona Orphan Abduction.* Cambridge: Harvard University Press, 2001.

Green, Justin. "Binky Brown Meets the Holy Virgin." In *Justin Green's Binky Brown Sampler*, San Francisco: Last Gasp, 1995.

Grimmelshausen, Johann. *Simplicissimus.* Translated by Mike Mitchell. Sawtry, UK: Dedalus, 2006.

Hansen, Miriam. "Early Cinema, Late Cinema: Permutations of the Public Sphere." *Screen* 34, no. 3 (1993): 197–210.

Harrigan, Pat, and Noah Wardrip-Fruin, eds. *Third Person: Authoring and Exploring Vast Narratives.* Cambridge: MIT Press, 2009.

Harvey, Robert C. *The Art of the Funnies: An Aesthetic History.* Jackson: University Press of Mississippi, 1993.

Horn, Maurice. *One Hundred Years of American Newspaper Comics.* New York: Gramercy, 1996.

Houellebecq, Michel. *H. P. Lovecraft: Against the World, against Life.* Translated by Dorna Khazeni. New York: McSweeney's, 2005.

In the Realms of the Unreal: The Mystery of Henry Darger. Directed by Jessica Yu. Los Angeles: Diorama Films, 2004.

Jablonski, Joseph. "Henry J. Darger: The Homer of the Mad." In *Surrealist Subversions: Rants, Writings & Images by the Surrealist Movement in the United States,* edited by Ron Sakolsky, 553–55. Brooklyn, NY: Autonomedia, 2002.

Juul, Jesper. *Half-Real: Video Games between Real Rules and Fictional Worlds.* Cambridge: MIT Press, 2005.

Klock, Geoff. *How to Read Superhero Comics and Why.* New York: Continuum, 2002.

Krasner, David. "Walter Benjamin and the Lynching Play: Mourning and Allegory in Angelina Weld Grimké's *Rachel.*" In *A Beautiful Pagent: African American Theatre, Drama, and Performance in the Harlem Renaissance, 1910–1927,* 97–111. New York: Palgrave Macmillan, 2002.

Lovecraft, H. P. *Amateur Journalism.* Vol. 1 of *Collected Essays.* Edited by S. T. Joshi. New York: Hippocampus, 2004.

———. *Tales.* Edited by Peter Straub. New York: Library of America, 2005.

MacGregor, John M. *Henry Darger: In the Realms of the Unreal.* New York: Delano Greenidge, 2002.

Mack, Arien. "Editor's Introduction." In "Martyrdom, Self-Sacrifice, and Self-Denial," ed. Arien Mack, special issue, *Social Research* 75, no. 2 (Summer 2008), xi–xii.

Markus, Deborah. "Realms of the Unreal: The Imaginary World of Henry Darger." *Spook* (July 2002) (http://www.nowherecity.com/people/thespook-2002–06k_nwc.pdf).

McDannell, Colleen. *Material Christianity: Religion and Popular Culture in America.* New Haven: Yale University Press, 1995.

Merleau-Ponty, Maurice. *The Visible and the Invisible.* Edited by Claude Lefort, translated by Alphonso Lingis. Evanston, IL: Northwestern University Press, 1968.

Moon, Michael. "The Gentle Boy from the Dangerous Classes: Pederasty, Domesticity, and Capitalism in Horatio Alger." *Representations* 19 (Summer 1987): 87–110.

Mooney, James. *The Ghost-Dance Religion and the Sioux Outbreak of 1890. 1896.* New York: Dover, 1991.

Negt, Oskar, and Alexander Kluge. *Public Sphere and Experience: Toward an Analysis of the Bourgeois and Proletarian Public Spheres.* Translated by Peter Labanyi, Jamie Owen Daniel, and Assenka Oksiloff. Minneapolis: University of Minnesota Press, 1993.

Nelson, Claudia. *Little Strangers: Portrayals of Adoption and Foster Care in America, 1850–1929.* Bloomington: Indiana University Press, 2003.

Payne, Mark. *Theocritus and the Invention of Fiction.* Cambridge, UK: Cambridge University Press, 2007.

Quinn, Seabury. *Alien Flesh.* Philadelphia: O. Train, 1977.

Riley, Michael O. *Oz and Beyond: The Fantasy World of L. Frank Baum.* Lawrence: University of Kansas Press, 1997.

Rosemont, Franklin, ed. *Surrealism and Its Popular Accomplices*. San Francisco: City Lights, 1980.

Rotella, Carlo. "Pulp History." *Raritan* 27, no. 1 (2007): 11–36.

Saitō, Tamaki. *Beautiful Fighting Girl*. Translated by J. Keith Vincent and Dawn Lawson. Minneapolis: University of Minnesota Press, 2011.

Sakolsky, Ron. "Introduction: Surrealist Subversion in Chicago." In *Surrealist Subversions: Rants, Writings & Images by the Surrealist Movement in the United States*, edited by Ron Sakolsky, 23–108. Brooklyn, NY: Autonomedia, 2002.

Santner, Eric L. *My Own Private Germany: Daniel Paul Schreber's Secret History of Modernity*. Princeton: Princeton University Press, 1996.

Sapir, Edward. "Psychiatric and Cultural Pitfalls in the Business of Getting a Living." 1939. In *Selected Writings of Edward Sapir in Language, Culture and Personality*, edited by David G. Mandelstam, 578–89. Berkeley: University of California Press, 1949.

Scheper-Hughes, Nancy. "The Global Traffic in Organs." *Current Anthropology* 41, no. 2 (2000): 191–224.

Schwartz, Sanford. "The Suspended Moment." *New York Review of Books*, February 10, 2000, 19–22.

Seldes, Gilbert. *The Seven Lively Arts*. 1924. New York: Dover, 2001.

Smith, Erin A. *Hard-Boiled: Working-Class Readers and Pulp Magazines*. Philadelphia: Temple University Press, 2000.

Warner, Marina. "Out of an Old Toy Chest." *Journal of Aesthetic Education* 43, no. 2 (2009): 10–12.

Williams, Linda. *Playing the Race Card: Melodramas of Black and White from Uncle Tom to O. J. Simpson*. Princeton: Princeton University Press, 2001.

ACKNOWLEDGMENTS

I am grateful to audiences at the talks I've given about Darger's work at The Johns Hopkins University; Emory University; the University of North Carolina, Chapel Hill; the Graduate Center at the City University of New York; Dartmouth College; Rutgers University; Concordia University, in Montreal; The Ohio State University; Indiana University; the University of Chicago; the University of Florida, Gainesville; the University of Maryland, College Park; and Manchester and York Universities in the United Kingdom, as well as to the colleagues who invited me to give those talks.

I also owe thanks to administrators at Johns Hopkins and Emory for the research leaves that have made it possible for me to complete this book.

I have never met the pioneering Darger researchers John MacGregor and Michael Bonesteel, but I feel personally grateful to them for their successful labors in recovering so much of what we now know about the outward circumstances of the artist's life. Although, as I discuss at some points in this book, I fundamentally disagree with several key aspects of MacGregor's interpretations of Darger's mind and behavior, I want to acknowledge fully my awareness of the considerable degree to which anyone undertaking extensive work on Darger's art and writing must be in MacGregor's debt. Again, like other students of Darger's work, I am indebted to Kiyoko Lerner and the late Nathan Lerner for their labors in preserving the work and in making it available to scholars, students, and the public. Brooke Davis Anderson, the longtime (now former) director and curator of the Contemporary Center of the American Folk Art Museum in New York, deserves the gratitude and admiration of everyone who cares about Darger's work for the generous care with which she discharged her responsibilities for overseeing the principal

Darger archive. I also wish to thank Andrew Edlin and Kendall Holland of the Andrew Edlin Gallery in New York for their generous help in obtaining the images of Darger's art reproduced in this book.

Christopher Nealon and Carol Mavor read and evaluated the manuscript for Duke University Press and offered generous and imaginative suggestions for improving it that made the last phase of revisions feel especially well supported. They have my lasting gratitude, as do Ken Wissoker, Jade Brooks, Rebecca Fowler, and their colleagues at Duke University Press. I thank Jeanne Ferris for her scrupulous copyediting and Amy Ruth Buchanan for her design of the book.

Besides the official readers, Lynne Huffer and Aaron Kunin also read a late version of the manuscript in its entirety and offered invaluable critical challenges and readerly support. Marcie Frank took the long journey with me and the book, reading it bit by bit as it emerged and offering good counsel about how the pieces (most of them, anyway) fit. Frequently exchanging work with Adam Frank, and discussing Gertrude Stein, Silvan Tomkins, composition, and affect with him, has helped me think further about Darger. Jared Gardner, a historian and connoisseur extraordinaire of graphic narrative, has provided invaluable material aid to this project, as have the blessed archivists at several institutions, including Courtney Wagner at the American Folk Art Museum, and Susan Liberator and Marilyn Scott at the Billy Ireland Cartoon Library & Museum at The Ohio State University. During his tenure as librarian at the American Folk Art Museum, James Mitchell made it possible for me to spend many hours reading Darger's writing.

Revisiting my childhood fascination with the legends of the early Roman martyrs and my (it turns out) by no means unrelated absorption in *Batman*, *Wonder Woman*, and *Classics Illustrated* comic books and many of the newspaper comic strips of the 1950s and 1960s has often reminded me of how much sharing these interests with my five siblings — Charlie, Tony, Bill, Eleanor, and Bob — intensified my joy in them. Thanks also to Julia Goldberg and Abby Goldberg for the (for me) enlivening interest they have taken in my work on Darger. Thanks to Millie Seubert for her sustaining friendship and for her generous and thoughtful responses to my writing in this and previous instances. Sylvia and Julian Ander have my loving gratitude for their intellectual and material hospitality to me and my thinking during these years; music I hear with them is more than music.

Veena Das's writing about violence and ordinary life and the plight of children under prolonged conditions of war has affected my work on Darger in more ways than I can say, and I thank her for the gift of her conversation about both my work and hers. I thank Lauren Berlant for challenging and fortifying conversations going back many years now.

Colin Talley, Elizabeth Wilson, Tamara Jones, and (again) Lynne Huffer have my deep appreciation for the ways in which they have made Atlanta an intellectual as well as an emotional home for me. A shout out to them, and to Michael Elliott, Craig Womack, and Allen Tullos, too, for their collegial friendship.

Nancy Gordon Seif has repeatedly and reliably helped me find and refind my place in life at critical moments (some of them lasting a good deal longer than a moment) over the past thirty years.

Late in the process of my writing this book, the world and I lost the peerless Eve Sedgwick. No words I can discover can do more than gesture toward saying how much the treasure of her questing and capacious spirit and brilliant and restless mind continues to enrich my life and that of many other people I love. Thanks to Hal Sedgwick as well as to many of Eve's and my former students for all they are doing to keep her legacy excitingly alive.

Jonathan Goldberg and I—despite our ripely mixed feelings about gay marriage and all that it implies—recently decided, after never having celebrated an anniversary before, to celebrate twenty-five years of being together. Here, again, words fail me, except for what I've already said in the dedication of this book to him. Beyond that, I'm going to have to rely on the soundtrack for help. (Cue up Richard Strauss, "Im Abendrot," *Four Last Songs*, in Lisa Della Casa's recording.)

INDEX

Darger, Henry (*continued*)

   of paintings by, 21–22; posthumous reputation, 22; as proletarian culture worker, 2–3; and principle of play, 3–5; and sexuality, 70–73

   paintings by:

   At Jennie Richee. While sending warning to their father, 12–15

   Untitled (Part 2 of 205), 16–18

   Untitled (The Arcadeia), xii–xvi

   writings by:

   In the Realms of the Unreal, 31–39, 70–71

Decamp, L. Sprague, 108

Dick Tracy (newspaper comic strip), 90

Don Quixote (Cervantes), 5

Emmerich, Anne, 114–15

Ewers, Hanns Heinz, 116

Fish, Albert, 120

Fisher, Bud, 94–95, 97–98

Foucault, Michel, 128

France, Anatole: *Revolt of the Angels*, 20

Gasoline Alley (newspaper comic strip), 90

Gein, Ed, 124–27

Gender change: in Baum's *Marvelous Land of Oz*, 8–9; in *In the Realms of the Unreal*, 8–9

Ghirlandaio, Domenico: *Massacre of the Innocents*, xii–xii; *Nativity of John the Baptist*, x–xii

Grimmelshausen, Johann: *Simplicissimus*, 133–34 n. 20, 135–36 n. 13

Happy Hooligan (newspaper comic strip), 88, 90

Heade, Martin Johnson: *Thunderstorm on Narragansett Bay*, 15–17

Henty, G. A.: *By Sheer Pluck: A Tale of the Ashanti War*, 64

Hitchcock, Alfred, 123–24

Howard, Robert, 107–12

James, William, 20

Klein, Melanie, 60–61, 109, 113

Kluge, Alexander: *See* Negt, Oskar

Little Annie Rooney (newspaper comic strip), 91–94

Little Orphan Annie (newspaper comic strip), 91

Lovecraft, H. P., 101–7

Lynching, 68–69

MacGregor, John M., 9, 11–12, 18–19, 38, 55–56, 70–73, 84, 127, 133 n. 18

Male genitals of girl figures, 9

Marston, William Moulton, 121–23

Martyr plays, 25–31

Massacre culture, 65–70

Masturbation, 71–75

Merleau-Ponty, Maurice, 102–3

Military chronicles: as model for Branwell Brontë's work, 63–65; as model for Darger's work, 44–45, 62–64

Mutt and Jeff (newspaper comic strip), 94–98

National Amateur Press Association, 139 n. 6

Negt, Oskar, and Alexander Kluge, 86, 131 n. 1

Payne, Mark, x

Pigtail (character in Brontë juvenilia), 69–70

Pilgrim's Progress (Bunyan), 5

"Plagiarism": etymology of term, 81

Proletarian public sphere, 20–21, 86–87, 108–9, 131 n. 1

Pulp fiction: and "pulp history," 107–12; "weird-horror" school of, 101. *See also* Howard, Robert; Lovecraft, H. P.

Quinn, Seabury, 115–16; *Alien Flesh*, 117–19

Racial difference: in Branwell Brontë's work, 65–67; in Darger's work, 132 n. 5
Radcliffe, Daniel (character in *In the Realms of the Unreal*, also known as the Rattle-snake Boy), 8
Roman Catholic devotional art, 27–28
Rotella, Carlo, 110–11

Saitō, Tamaki, 9–10
Santner, Eric, 76–77
Schloeder, William (friend of Darger), 4, 6–7, 82, 88–89

Sequels and sequelation, 7, 10–12
Sissyish behavior, 38–39
Superman (comic-book character), 113

Trauerspiel (mourning play), 40–41
Turmer, Jennie (character in *In the Realms of the Unreal*), 38–39

Uncle Tom's Cabin (Stowe), 5–6

Violence, 60–61, 69, 109

Warburg, Aby, x–xii
Wertham, Fredric, 120–21
Wilde, Oscar, 68–69
Williams, Linda, 5
Wonder Woman (comic-book character), 121–23; and bondage and discipline, 121–22

MICHAEL MOON IS A PROFESSOR IN THE
GRADUATE INSTITUTE OF THE LIBERAL
ARTS AT EMORY UNIVERSITY.

Library of Congress Cataloging-in-Publication Data
Moon, Michael, 1950–
Darger's resources / Michael Moon.
p. cm.
Includes bibliographical references and index.
ISBN 978-0-8223-5142-9 (cloth : alk. paper)
ISBN 978-0-8223-5156-6 (pbk. : alk. paper)
1. Darger, Henry, 1892–1972. 2. Artists—United
States—Biography. 3. Art and popular culture—
United States—History—20th century. I. Title.
NX512.D37M66 2012
700.92—dc23
[B]
2011041909

www.ingramcontent.com/pod-product-compliance
Lightning Source LLC
Chambersburg PA
CBHW072139170526
45158CB00004BA/1431